Do You Speak Equis?

Communicative Interactions using the Headcollar and Bit

Do You Speak Equis?
Communicative Interactions using the Headcollar and Bit

Antonello Radicchi

Translated by Julie de Joncaire Narten

J.A. ALLEN

First published in 2017 by
JA Allen

JA Allen is an imprint of
The Crowood Press Ltd
Ramsbury, Marlborough
Wiltshire SN8 2HR

www.crowood.com

British Library Cataloguing-in-Publication Data
A catalogue record for this book is available from the British Library.

ISBN 978 1 908809 60 5

Photos
All photos, including the cover are the property of ©Francesco Busignani, except
the following: Page 13 Michelangelo Buonarroti, *The Creation of Adam* (detail),
1508-1512; Pages 16, 19, 30, 34, 35, 37, 49 Drawings by Carlo De Joncaire Narten;
Pages 69, 70, 76, 77, 78, 79, 80, 161 ©Antonello Radicchi Schemi tecnici; Page 16
©Antonello Radicchi; Page 103 Fossil of Marrella splendens. Released under the GNU
Free Documentation License; Page 104 Haikouella lanceolata. Creative Commons.
Wikipedia.org-User: Archaeodontosaurus

Translation from the Italian: Julie de Joncaire Narten

Disclaimer
The content of this book is the author's opinion only. The author and publisher
shall have neither liability nor responsibility to any person or entity with respect to
any damage or injury caused or alleged to be caused directly or indirectly by the
information contained in this book. JA Allen encourages the use of approved safely
helmets in all equestrian sports and activities.

Typeset by Jean Cussons Typesetting, Diss, Norfolk

Printed and bound in India by Replika Press Pvt Ltd

Contents

Acknowledgements

If only I could steadfastly hold on to my principles without ever being untrue to myself … but I am only a little man accompanied by a great hope, which leads me by the hand when I get lost. This is a hymn to hope, the only certainty in life!

To all those who have helped me write this book, who have shared the hard climbs, the vertiginous descents, and the desolate plains all the way to our comfortable clearings – to all of you I can only say 'thank you', which hardly expresses my feelings. So to all those who know me, I simply ask that you look for the gratitude in my eyes each time I look at you. I am certain that you will see it.

To Count Antonio Bolza, Count Benedikt, Donna Nencia, with whom I have shared much. To Catia and Silvia – how lucky I am to have met them. To the man who freezes the moment, Francesco Busignani, assisted by Samuele Radicchi, who will forever be squabbling over the right to be called 'Trinity'. To our translator Julie de Joncaire Narten and to Carlo de Joncaire Narten, producer of the drawings, who have taken this project so much to heart. To Gianni Gamberini and Alberto Capogreco, who corrected and edited the book. Carlotta De, Alice Arcangeli, Sara la Grassa, Bruno Dorigo, Irene Boriosi, Noeme Statuti. To the Divine Matilde … (I add nothing more). To my muse and companion Maria Francesca Patrizi.

To them, who have given me so much, asking only for understanding in exchange. To them, to the horses I have encountered and will encounter in my life. In the knowledge that I will never be worthy of them but that I will never be able to do without them.

Introduction

'The measure of intelligence is the ability to change.'

ALBERT EINSTEIN

Money, without sacrifice, cannot buy culture or learning. But it may well purchase horses and equipment, rendering the horseman poorer than he thinks he is.

ANTONELLO RADICCHI

RESCHIO

An array of emotions overwhelming the senses, one after the other! Sight, first of all, unveils the views whose real beauty is then confirmed by touch in a more direct and tangible way, in the way that Reschio was in fact first conceived and developed. Believe me, it is difficult to describe the concrete beauty of such a place, beautiful in all its honesty. I could describe its centuries-old trees, the houses, which although luxurious, are humbly led to the altar, to marry an unspoiled environment, creating a union of harmonious and perfect shapes. Everything is like this; all has been conceived as if it were the natural result of its realization. That house is there because nothing else could be. If I drew a perfect picture in my head, I would do nothing other than repeat exactly what I see there. There is no need to think 'maybe if …' or 'maybe it would have been better …'. No, it's perfect; I wouldn't change a single thing. I

The stables at Reschio.

wasn't surprised by forms or striking details – in fact, the first time I set foot in Reschio, I was surprised not to be surprised. The sensation that I would like to describe is that of being fully aware that everything there is not common, but so indispensable that it should be. How often do we thank those we love for loving us …? But how nice and indispensable it is to be loved … and especially if you feel loved by something really wonderful and sincere, then it would be hard not to fall in love. The point is, that to live in such an environment is all too easy, but to conceive it, certainly a little less. The Bolza family were able to do it, firstly the Count Antonio Bolza and then his son Benedikt. The thought of conceiving an idea so simple and at the same time so 'huge' frightens and amazes me. Clearly it is not the idea that frightens me, far from it, but its implementation. We all have beautiful ideas, but how many of these become reality? They require courage, faith and perseverance over time.

Why am I writing all this? And, moreover, what has it got to do with the language of horses?

Life is surely made up of encounters, places and people who leave a deep mark on our existence whether good or bad. Count Antonio Bolza for me is certainly a very important person and Reschio is a very important place. In fact all the studies and the techniques that I developed are none other than a consequence of this meeting. I would never have been able to make such in-depth studies without his support. Developing new theories and new systems of communication requires time, concentration and collaboration.

This adventure began fifteen years ago. At that time I had started to learn the techniques and concepts in lightness from the maestro Philippe Karl, whilst Count Antonio Bolza was just starting out in equitation, but we didn't yet know each other. Our paths crossed when Count Bolza called on me to resolve some of the problems he was having with his horses. Reschio

Count Antonio Bolza on Casanova di Reschio.

was already a reality but the stud farm didn't yet exist. I was working in my riding centre in Umbria about 40km from Reschio.

The lightness techniques appealed to Count Bolza and we began to see each other more frequently until, one evening, after a lesson, driven by the same 'insane' passion for horses, we began to talk about starting a small stud farm. We both had clear ideas on what the 'ideal' horse should be; the problem was how to find one.

We would need a rather elastic and harmonious horse, like an Iberian, but at the same time he should be strong and solid like a German one. Count Bolza asked me if there were pure-bred horses with such characteristics, without cross- breeding. I replied that we could begin a search starting from the breed characteristics that we would like to preserve as dominant. Undoubtedly, he would prefer a horse that had dominant characteristics of elasticity. I could only agree with such an idea!

Then, we decided, our next stop would be Spain.

Do you know the old saying 'There's many a slip twixt cup and lip'. Well, never has a saying been truer. To keep things short, we went to Spain and visited innumerable stud farms but it appeared that our horse had not yet been born. We saw many beautiful, elegant horses, but they were always too baroque. There is nothing wrong with horses with those characteristics; I personally adore them, but we wanted something different, something much closer to the concept of a 'sport' horse. Certainly our idea was ambitious and how many before us had thought of it …? But, as I said before, an idea remains just that, until it is transformed into reality and, often, mere willpower is not sufficient to make that happen. Faith is needed and, if you wish, a bit of luck. So, on the last day of our stay, we went to visit the last stud farm on our programme. It was the prestigious breeding centre of the Candaù family.

There he was – I remember it as if it were just yesterday, Uranio VI, a magnificent four-year-old grey stallion 17.2 hands high, built slightly 'uphill', powerful haunches, correct shoulders; neither too oblique nor too upright, perfect neck-line, quite long but not at all heavy, a high, light head, with a proud gaze … we couldn't believe our eyes. The next question was: 'how will he move?' He was fabulous, harmonious, with the right amount of extension and elevation. He was perfect, the horse for whom we had searched so long. Not only this, but, at the same stud farm, we also found a mare who had similar characteristics.

Uranio VI, progenitor of the Reschio stud-farm.

*Donna Nencia
Corsini on Il
Magnifico.*

Of course we selected another three brood mares to see the ancestry, but our main idea proved to be correct, that is, Uranio VI with Lentisca. This was the solid base for our breeding. An idea that became reality.

Il Magnifico was the name chosen for the first foal born at Reschio. Many more followed: Aurora, Magnolia, Punto, Cassandra, Serenissimo … I can't remember exactly when, but at a certain point at Reschio, there were at least forty horses descended for the main part from Uranio. And so our little group of brood mares started to grow and became a herd of more than fifteen individuals lovingly cared for under the centuries-old trees in the hilly pastures of the 'earldom of Reschio' (as I like to call it). The herd brought us great riches, clearly not of the economic kind; whoever has or has had breeding experience knows that the decision, indeed the improvised madness that brings a person of sane mind to undertake such a journey, is driven largely by passion and results in a lot of spent money. Often the only profit is the privilege of spending time with one's horses. No, the wealth I received from the herd was of another kind. It was the opportunity to observe and, after a lot of observing, maybe to sense the grammatical structure of the language of the horse and to appreciate its blatant simplicity and concreteness. The harmonic whisper, or impetuous gesture of authority, the loving touch, the patient tolerance, the hierarchical rebellions, the sense of belonging, the collective consciousness, the consciousness of oneself …. Without the herd, without watching it repeatedly and continuously, it would be difficult to understand. It requires a lot of time to start to sense, to understand, to start to speak, to express oneself in a fitting way. I can't remember how much time I spent in watching them. In summer I would sit myself under an old oak tree at the top edge of the pasture, in the hottest hours of the day, when it was impossible to ride. I remained there with a sandwich and a bottle of water, sometimes napping, in good company, sharing with them the heat, the sultry air and the insects. Every moment I could, I escaped to my little corner of paradise. I often brought many of my texts on ethology with me, searching for a direct confirmation of what I was reading. Books helped me, but the herd taught and educated me. Unlike money, the type of wealth that I received never runs out – indeed the more it is spent and used the more it increases. The best investment is always the one made on ourselves. Don't take your horse to be trained, or rather do, but find a person who can help you, but, above all, help you understand, how to do and how to make the horse do.

A good instructor is not one who makes the horse do complex exercises, but one who can transmit his own art to other people as well as to the horse. In this way the work bears fruit, otherwise it is and will always remain a sterile gratification of one's ego. Gratification is important, but not fundamental, in that it creates competition and competition goes arm-in-arm with the ego, which doesn't train us, but just claims to. I say this because I fall into this trap every time I have to prepare a horse for a competition. In the end I will learn. I will learn to do this whilst always respecting the horse. Perhaps I will learn … competition is an ugly beast, really difficult to keep under control, at times useful, but often damaging. Useful in that it pushes one to improve; dangerous because it can lead one to constrain. At least that's the way I look at it.

Don't think, however, that everything was a bed of roses; we had to endure many storms, some of which seriously tried to sink us. The biggest storm came about a year after the horses arrived at Reschio. Uranio suffered a clostridial muscular infection in his right hind leg from a simple injection, which left him with permanent mechanical lameness.

Nevertheless, with the supervision of veterinarians, we continued to work the horse. He managed to carry out all the dressage movements with ease but with an evident mechanical lameness, which could only be seen in walk.

I take this opportunity to thank all the staff led by Dr Marco Pepe at the University Clinic of Perugia, who worked with their hearts as well as their intellect, saving the life of the horse. Clearly he couldn't take part in sporting competitions, but we still had our stallion and the pride in his gaze never left us. Pride which I have seen many times in his offspring, including

The Reschio Herd.

in Orlando di Reschio, who died two years ago from colic at the clinic of Perugia. He was eight years old and was ready for competition.

> *Orlando, I can say that you were the most beautiful and honest horse I have ever had and you will never return. It breaks my heart every time I think of you.*

If life could ever return something to me, if I could make only one wish, I would like to have my horse back, because he was, to all effects, 'my' horse. He belonged to me, in the noblest sense of the word. Never in my life have I felt such intense pain for a non-human being. Pain that I feel even today, and, I am convinced, will remain with me for the rest of my life.

Leaving storms aside, there were many happy moments shared with Count Bolza, who has always helped and supported me in my work. And when I say helped, I mean that he was always ready to get his hands dirty whenever needed, never holding back, managing with great sacrifice and strength of will to learn new training techniques, often mounting lively youngsters or horses in an advanced level of work, mastering the technique, and in the end he himself becoming the main source of learning for his horses. I owe all my respect to a person who approached this world at fifty-five years of age, showing a technique and an innate sensitivity beyond the norm. I just wanted to say that most of the techniques described in this book and consequently their experimentation, took place at Reschio: as well as the development and sharing of them that occurred with Count Antonio Bolza.

Count Antonio Bolza on Baron De Lis, Antonello Radicchi on Casanova.

Contact is the principle on which communication, all interaction and sequences of events are based. It is everything.

WITH TACT

Change and mutation are the forces that are driving us, and to unharness ourselves is impossible, at least in the world I know or that I believe I know. This forces us to evolve, in fact, to return to the primary need to communicate.

We men have great difficulty in communicating with each other and even more so with our inner selves. We are unable to understand ourselves, yet presume to understand the next person without the slightest notion of the facts or the necessary means to penetrate the human soul, at times straying beyond the comprehensible and losing sight of the understanding already acquired by our often forgotten and undervalued empirical heritage. In brief, we look up at the peaks, beautifully luminous and full of mystery, forgetting where our feet are planted. To untangle oneself from all these sensations is often a difficult but not impossible undertaking if one manages to establish a 'contact'. I will speak of 'contact' before moving on to 'communication' *per se* because contact is the most important thing: the basic link that ties beings and, though very variable and unstable, it becomes equally reliable once we have mastered it.

It needs time, care and an ongoing commitment in refining the senses of feeling, and all our initial efforts must be lavished on the development of this, which is more or less deeply rooted inside each one of us. It is up to us to explore it and develop its infinite capabilities. Without this well-developed ability, all our efforts to understand, act or impart instructions will be useless.

But what is contact? Contact is the essence of feeling, of knowing, and of understanding. It is the principle on which communication, all future interaction and sequence of events are based.
Simply put, contact is everything!

The best definition and one that raises another fundamental concept, is perhaps obtained by splitting the Italian word for contact (*contatto*) and translating and analysing its component parts individually: *con* meaning 'with'; *tatto* meaning 'tact', which is what we have to use to obtain it.

In fact we need to use *tact* and taking away the space between the words, in Italian we arrive at *con-tact*.

> *With tact, with-tact, contact. The awareness of feeling and being felt.*

If there is no contact, there is no communication and without communication there is no rapport. But if the contact, as often happens, is too strong, it is extremely damaging and, even though we may not want to, it causes innumerable sufferings to, and adversely affects, our horse.

We are not perfect and therefore we will make mistakes. To err is part of our learning process, but to understand and recognize our own mistakes is the basis of growth and development towards a closer and friendlier rapport based on respect.

To understand contact and to develop it, we must initially understand what the horse feels; how and when he feels it. It is important to understand the 'how' –that is, which methods we can use to establish contact through our actions.

CHAPTER 1

The Primary Requirement – Energy

Energy is precious for all living beings and all living beings have an awareness of this, except one; man. We are not speaking of electric energy or renewable sources, which is another subject, but of the energy we need to move, to breathe, to survive, to overcome disease and, in the case of horses, their predators. We are speaking of the food from which this energy can be obtained, which is easily available at the supermarket and rather less so in nature.

Let's imagine the case of a wild herd. Those who will have the best chance of surviving the cold or predators are those who, in identical conditions, will have available to them a larger energy supply on which they can draw in times of difficulty; in fact a horse with a good layer of fat can tolerate the cold more easily than a thin and malnourished horse, who will find it difficult to pass the winter.

Energy and food are linked.

Energy and food are linked. By nature, a horse spends most of his time eating or looking for food, which is a precious thing and the awareness of this is, for the horse, logical and natural. Much less natural is feeding 'rations', which obliges the horse to eat concentrated meals (feed) and measures of 'forage' (a little hay). We content ourselves with giving our friends the correct calorific provisions without taking into account the way the horse is used to consuming them.

Apparently, our habits are rational: if we give the horse concentrated feed, we might then reduce the total amount of hay and, in so doing, we have two big advantages; the first is that we will need less storage space for hay and the second is that the horse will pass fewer droppings, having less quantity of waste to expel. The negative aspect of all this is that we de-naturalize the horse, keeping him closed in a box or small paddock, therefore no longer with a herd or social rapport, without regular access to grazing, and therefore nothing to do for days, weeks, months or even years. We have thus created a favourable environment for the development of depressive pathologies, which will then be the cause of stress with all the consequences connected to it, such as cribbing, weaving and so on. The horse should eat in an almost continuous manner, never without hay but always having it slightly in excess, especially in cases where social life is totally or almost totally absent. This topic is linked to language even if it doesn't seem apparent, but it is, inasmuch as we can never understand language without a deep awareness of the mechanics of its existence and therefore of all the mechanisms associated with it. This awareness in fact reveals something really important that we can use as leverage during our training of the horse. **The horse tends to conserve energy and it is not natural for him to waste it: as a consequence, it will guide us on how to act.**

For example: in training we can say that short exercises will be the most efficient, hence those that we interrupt immediately every time they have been correctly executed. We will be certain, that with this method, we will impress a really clear message in the horse's mind so that he will gladly do this again under identical conditions. We should continue to ask and to put him under pressure until we begin to have his response channelled in the desired direction (he will show us the intention of doing), then immediately cease to ask **(yielding), bringing him back into a 'comfortable situation'.**

Now, we know that this mechanism works, but moreover we also know why and from whence it derives: from the unconscious need to save energy.

We must not make the mistake of confusing all of this with laziness. I don't mean this at all – in that laziness is the consequence of bad training and of faulty communication: lazy horses do not exist, but badly educated ones do. The natural attitude of the horse to conserve energy

is fundamental to having a horse with good impulsion and ready willingness, but we will look at this aspect in more detail later on as, at this point, we are still missing too many elements without which it will be impossible to understand.

The horse tends to conserve energy and it is not natural for him to waste it.

CHAPTER 2

The Herd and Private Property

To be part of a herd is rather like living in a small village where everyone knows everything about everyone else and where everyone is useful but no one is indispensable.

Hierarchy and respect are the cornerstones of the law of the herd, which all members respect through an education imparted to them from the first days of life. Every member has a well-defined social position of which they are aware, as they are aware of the social position of every other member; knowing to whom an individual owes respect and from whom he should receive it. A concept that has helped me to understand this, is that if 'Frank is dominated by Julie and Julie is in turn dominated by Louis, it doesn't absolutely follow that Louis dominates Frank'.

Each horse has a private property, which he takes with him wherever he goes. The dimensions depend on the location, on his social position and the circumstances. This property is

Each horse has a private property, which it takes with it wherever it goes.

off-limits to members of a lower position and intrusions are not normally tolerated unless authorized, whilst it is largely ignored by members who occupy a higher social position. This same property will, however, always be protected even from higher-ranking individuals, not by defending its boundaries but simply by moving it elsewhere, far enough away from the boundaries of the more commanding members. If a horse enters the living space of another who is superior to him, this could lead to a physical confrontation, but for this to happen he would have had to ignore all the warning signs and therefore the pressures which are increasingly manifested:

- Look
- Attitude
- Attempt at aggression
- And finally, aggression

The really important thing for us to note is that these signals, except in special cases, are given in a progressive way and are immediately interrupted once acknowledged.

I emphasize: interrupted as soon as acknowledged.

All of this goes back to the first law: the primary need to 'save energy'; don't do more than you need to. It serves no purpose for you to shout if I hear you! But with horses we are always shouting and often show aggression before warning. We are not consistent with their way of communicating, and yet we seek to interact with them, expecting that they adapt to us and, contrary to what we may think, they adapt to our requests/inducements and they do so more often than we imagine.

But there's a limit beyond which the adaptation or adjustment fails to bring benefits and it will therefore become sterile and illogical to go on, inducing as a consequence, rebellion, non-collaboration or insensitivity to commands; all of this because we don't understand each other.

If we are the more evolved species it is up to us to study and understand.

Isn't that simple? Study in order to understand, to learn, to communicate, but we hardly ever do so. Why not? Laziness and pride are the main factors. There are books, studies and logic that would lead us to understand and conclude that the continued and widespread use of archaic, violent and constrictive methods of training will indeed make us the masters: but only of the ignorance that enriches merchants, always ready to rob our cultural wealth in exchange for bits that purport to give miraculous results; or the many instructors for whom it is easier, more remunerative and far less strenuous, to convince us to change horses because the one we have doesn't work and we deserve something more, something better, more suited to our ability. Our ego emerges victorious. Hooray!

CHAPTER 3

Communicative Action and Receptive Reaction

Through actions we obtain reactions. This gives us the first parameter, that is, when the horse begins to feel. We can perceive this by observing each tiny change of state caused by our interaction, whatever it may be, provided that it has caused a change, a reaction.

We have said that contact is when we start to feel each other but, not being initially able to communicate verbally, expecting logical answers, we must accustom ourselves to observe the reactions which are the only signals the horse will give us and these will be our yardstick.

Contact is not 'to touch' as we so often picture it in our mind, or at least it's not a physical touch in itself but rather the awareness of being felt. In short, especially for the horse, physical contact is not necessary for him to feel us or to enter into contact with us. Indeed, initially, physical contact can be too violent or traumatic for the sensitivity of a horse.

The compression of a wall of air between us and the horse is more than sufficient to cause him to run off. Therefore contact may or may not be physical, but it is that precise situation in which the horse begins to perceive our active presence expressed, or in other words, given to us, demonstrated, evidenced, by an acknowledging attitude.

The horse can perfectly feel a fly on his haunches and that he may then decide to ignore it or to tolerate it doesn't mean that he hasn't felt it. His sensitivity far exceeds our imagination and therefore, in order to understand this, we need to make a great effort to expand the margins of our comprehension.

Contact is not a physical touch in itself but rather the awareness of being felt. Physical touch is not necessary for the horse to feel us or to enter into contact with us.

A BIT OF PRACTICE IN OBSERVATION

Having the opportunity to observe the natural behaviour of the horse in the herd, without interacting, is the basis of understanding.

Of course it's not easy but neither is it impossible; we don't need a huge herd but just a nucleus composed of specimens possibly of different ages and extraction; mares, foals and so on. The sensation that one has after a period of observation is that there is always active communication inside the herd. A mild and subdued communication, made of well-defined attitudes that are occasionally reinforced, but only for the shortest of time when the need arises to educate or re-establish hierarchy.

Rarely is physical contact resorted to, only when all the other signals have been ignored. Physical contact, the imparting of physical pain, is allowed and is part of the herd, but usually this is not necessary and the *objective is always to re-establish communication, intended as a reaction to a mild contact based on a non-violent but respectful level. Violence is never an end in itself or gratuitous.*

This gives us the basis for understanding that interaction based on progressive acceptance of collaboration is not only possible, since the horse tends towards such behaviour, but is desirable.

For stallions with whom I have always worked, things tend to be quite different, but never as far as sensitivity is concerned. We will speak of this further on.

Usually, a stallion needs time to begin to collaborate in a constant way. It is normal for him to try to reach a dominant position in order to be able to pass on his genes. Because of this, his attempts at dominance are never completely dormant. As a consequence, more time is needed to be able to attain his collaboration in a constant way, and the fact that today we succeed in having it is not a guarantee that tomorrow we may not have to start all over again. In the light of these facts, we must not fall into the trap of being led to believe that a stallion is less sensitive or that he doesn't understand; he simply has different priorities and these

To be part of a herd is a bit like living in a small village where everyone knows everything about everyone else, and where everyone is useful, but no-one is indispensable.

priorities lead to consequent behaviours. These basic needs, clearly, can be more or less strong depending on the subjects, on their age, on experiences and so on. All this doesn't change the underlying sensitivity of the communicative relationship and 'stronger' actions are not needed in interaction with them. We only need more time for gaining their attention and more care from us in keeping it constant.

The Maestro Philippe Karl says that if a horse could choose, he would choose lightness. I would permit myself to add that he does this as it is a fundamental part of being a horse, rooted in the essence of his very language as a rewarding objective and positive consequence of harmony.

The crucial point of all this is to find the intrinsic sensitivity of each horse and on this, and only this, base our choices. Not, as often happens, base them on our own sensitivities, which are almost never appropriate to theirs, or on our needs, which are not those of the horse.

If we believe ourselves, rightly or wrongly, to be a more advanced species than the horse, then it is up to us to meet the horses and adapt to their language, to understand it, apply it, then use it to our advantage to bring them to a higher state of collaboration. It should never be to the contrary, especially at the beginning – which is something we often demand.

The horse is not a stupid or intelligent animal: he is a horse! … with all that this entails.

We human beings have reached this point in evolution and we have within us, transmitted by our ancestors, a strong spirit of adaptation dictated by the changing conditions of the environment, the climate and all the variables to which we have been subjected during the course of evolution. Adaptation is at the base of life, of course, within certain fixed limits.

Therefore, the horse often adapts, tolerates, endures, but he can only do so within certain limits. However, all of this is very far from education. To educate is to find the best and more natural route to make the horse learn, understand and execute.

In our world, we have to agree that mankind can't bend nature and other human beings to his own exigencies. Lately though, things have begun to take a different turn. Evolution seems to have changed gear and for the first time in history, mankind is radically changing the environment to adapt it to himself.

Find the intrinsic sensitivity of each horse and base your choices on this, rather than our own inappropriate needs.

INVERSE RELATIONSHIP

I have mentioned, speaking of contact, that because of our lack of sensitivity and receptiveness to body language, it could initially seem difficult for us to fully understand its effectiveness. When it was explained to me for the first time that a horse is aware of our every minimal change of state, I was certain I had understood. However, when I was shown how a horse reacts during ground work, going from walk to halt, at the tiniest hint of movement from the shoulders of his trainer, I could hardly believe my eyes. It was simply inconceivable. And not only did he execute the halt, he set off again, changed direction and so on. If this was possible, and it was, there was an enormous, immense and unrecognized receptive potential. And if this receptive potential existed, it meant that, up to that moment, I, or rather my horse, was trying to communicate with an idiot who had the sensitivity of a pneumatic drill – a bit like having a relationship with a steam-iron! Immediately I began to think that, if a horse could sense the movement of a wall of air between us, what effect were my hands having messing around in the inside of his mouth through the snaffle bit or worse? I couldn't bear to think of it. I began to be aware of the enormous suffering that I was causing him and I went a long time without riding, trying to limit my interactions with him to the minimum.

But this was not going to work. I had to find a solution. And this was how I began to get interested in ethology and luckily I found some wonderful people along the road.

Let it be clear that one learns much more, spending a day observing a herd, than reading the best treatise ever written on ethology, as long as one has some awareness of what one should be observing. The more one trains oneself to do so, the more things will reveal themselves; things that have always been there, but which one was never able to see.

Often we struggle to get in touch with that part of us that is essential to reaching an acceptable level of interaction in a natural way and not modified by standard human behaviour. We find ourselves enveloped in the mists of an evolution so drastic that it always leads us to modify the environment more and more and adapt it to our needs, while all other living beings constantly strive to adapt to it. Consequently at this level of development, we find it increasingly difficult to adapt. No one these days would get lost in a city. Thousands of signs and neon lights are there communicating with us, searching for our attention, or to sell us something. We are bombarded with more and more intense and numerous messages that pollute, disfigure and confuse our senses. We are completely desensitized. Alone, in a wood, many of us would be panicked. Yet even in the wood there are clear signs. The problem is that we are no longer used to reading them. For example, it should be enough to observe a tree and to note on which side the moss grows to be able to understand approximately which way north is. Why aren't we able to do this anymore? Simply, because it is no longer necessary: we don't need to do it. Consequently, on a developmental level, we have increasing difficulty in adapting because we are used to adapting the environment to us, to accommodate our needs. Instead, a horse, even if beaten, mistreated, who bites, bucks and kicks, can, in a single day, find calm and serenity, radically changing his attitude with a mere change in conditions. For a human, this would take years of therapy, which is often ineffective.

Another important point to consider is the genetic difference between prey and predator in terms of awareness and attention. In nature, prey must obviously maintain their attention and be almost constantly alert. On the other hand predators struggle to maintain their attention or constant concentration for more than forty-five minutes. For this reason, since one can hardly expect horses to change their status from prey to predator, we will need to open the door to a deeper understanding of what it means to be prey, on all levels. We will have to let them educate us, re-educating our way of seeing things, looking at them from a different point of view, re-educating our bodies and training our reactions to be in line with those of horses. We are slow; our instincts and our senses have dozed off; adapting to our style of life and the effort that is required of us goes against our nature and the most impervious obstacle to surmount will be our predatory ego. At this point it is clear that the more we respect horses' way of being, the less we respect ours, but we do it out of love, understanding or simply opportunism. We will do it, but let's not even mention natural methods since, as a matter of fact, it is everything but natural, at least not for us, who have to transform ourselves from predator to prey. An inverse relationship. For us it is more natural to be what we are. If we were to use our instinct, dormant as it may be, we would certainly achieve a more immediate reaction, but we can't do this. It would guide us as predators and, even if we managed to reach a rapport of dominance and submission, which might initially seem efficient, we would not manage to arrive at true collaboration because the horse would be too afraid to trust us. To concentrate, not to react instinctively, to express ourselves with body language, to read and translate this language, to interpret it – all of this requires, as well as good concentration, time.

The problem is that time, whilst we are interacting, is a luxury that we can't afford.

Time is an integral part of the very language, made up of action-reaction, from which it derives its meaning. We have to train ourselves to converse and to express ourselves through our body, to concentrate and visualize what it is that we are trying to ask, and try to predict possible reactions. The horse will be ready as he always is and we cannot be unprepared. If we learn to see, experience will teach us.

To think that applied ethology in training cannot be violent is a mere nonsense; always assuming that by violence one didn't mean the mere physical nature of the act. There is violence that occurs on a mental level that can be much more ferocious than a physical one. Therefore the famous gentle training can become a requirement for submission, not expressed in physical terms but expressed by controlling the psychological behaviour of the horse, which, if badly applied, can become more dangerous than physical submission, in that it can deeply affect the horse's mental parameters. To know, to understand, to apply is all that we can do; to educate is by no means simple and it is therefore always a route to be undertaken with awareness, without which this type of discipline is just a powerful weapon and, like all weapons, potentially dangerous.

OBSERVATION

How does a horse express himself? How does he reveal his feelings?
What is it that is easily understood or evident to us?

It will seem strange, but one thing that all mammals have in common, and therefore also horses, is facial mimicry. Conversely, ethologists have discovered that almost all types of marsupials, such as kangaroos, that don't use these muscles to suckle at the breast because the milk is delivered via an internal pump, are completely without facial expressions. They thus appear to our senses to be cold and unpredictable at every change, going from a tranquil state to one of aggression without any apparent manifestation in their faces. In reality I am sure that even they send out evident signals that we don't yet understand. It's a bit like when we listen to the radio – we manage to hear it without perceiving the sound waves.

The horse, of course, is not a kangaroo and even less a radio, but he is something very close to our primordial way of being and acting. Part of the language through which the

How does a horse express himself?

horse expresses himself was often used by us in the past before ours gradually evolved into its current form.

It is a part of us, dormant, forgotten, but an integral part of our primitive language, that often, without realizing it, we still use today. The important thing to bear in mind is that the horse, unlike us, is not ambiguous, two-faced or false and, contrary to us, cannot convey joy if he feels angry.

We can say 'Hi, How pleased I am to bump into you' when in reality we are thinking 'why didn't I take a different route …' The horse can't. He is not capable of doing it because his body and mind are so closely linked that his mental attitude always influences his physical attitude and *consequently a physical attitude, has a very strong influence on changing a mental attitude.*

This means that, if a horse is mentally excited, and therefore displays the physical characteristics of such a state, if we manage, with the use of the language (we will see how) to bring him to a physical attitude of calm and serenity, like having a stretched neck, low head and so on, such an attitude will tend also to influence his mental state, since it is so deeply and indissolubly linked to his physicality.

'Things are what they appear' and also 'Change the appearance, and you change the essence.'

In the same way that a mental attitude influences the physical, a physical attitude influences the mind, and all of this is fascinating.

The horse is a simple being, extremely sensitive, but simple! For us aspiring educators, this entails an even greater commitment and that is, to understand how a horse 'works' from a biomechanical point of view, but for the moment, let us understand what tools we have available to us to enable interaction.

As humans, we are 'prehensile' predators. We take, we grab, we squeeze … all things that are antagonistic to the nature of the horse. The more we squeeze our hands tight, the more the horse's trust and collaboration slip through our fingers and soon we end up with a closed, empty fist screaming our frustration to the wind and the gods.

Our concept of pulling or grabbing to bring closer, or pushing to move away, needs a severe revision.

I have said that we have facial mimicry in common with horses. It is relatively simple to recognize aggressive attitudes in them, such as ears back – mouth open – bared teeth – neck stretched out in attack mode. This is an easily recognizable place from which to start.

The problem now is to refine all this, until we can perceive things that are less evident to our senses, but without which our journey would stop at a level that would be far from being effective.

Let's turn back in our minds to how a horse behaves himself in nature: rather let's go further; let's try to immerse ourselves in the role of a member of the herd. Let us feel part of it, initially as an observer, and then afterwards, when we are a bit more knowledgeable, as an active member of this herd. The herd, as mentioned, has a social hierarchical structure, within which the roles are well defined even though they may change, depending on the dominant characters and the extent to which these tend to emerge or maintain their status.

But let's proceed in order.

Each horse, within the herd, has a well-defined role (even if partly changeable), and every horse within the herd knows perfectly well what his role is: he knows how to recognize those individuals who occupy a higher or lower hierarchical position to his own; is aware of himself as well others and their roles. Each individual tends to lead or be led according to the genes present in his DNA and may have sympathies or antipathies, therefore attaching himself more or less to other members of the herd.

A leader tends to lead, earning respect; a follower tends to follow, to be submissive and give respect. The characteristics of a leader are to go up the grades and the characteristics of a follower are those of following and submission.

Usually, it is the oldest mares who are the leaders, but not always. It often happens that the strongest subjects, physically and mentally, tend to become the point of reference and affirm themselves as such irrespective of age – which is, however, a fundamental parameter. There are various grades of leader and various grades of followers.

To learn the language, we have to understand a bit more about the dynamics and the components that make the horse what he is. One of these things is space and how horses relate to it, which we will now try to understand from their point of view.

CHAPTER 4

Space

For a horse, space is a complex and fundamental subject. To live in a herd does not mean to live piled on top of each other, or at least not always.

To live in a herd means to earn the right to one's own living space and this space is defended every time it is threatened.

Space means food, that is a part of the environment where grass grows, and that grass is life. Space means the ability to move suddenly when there is danger, and then to regroup once on the run, becoming one body with a huge mass. But, for the first few metres, to have space can mean not being trampled or not being hindered in movement, even if later on the group tends to cling back together to increase the sense of protection from predators. A horse's space will be all the larger, the greater his intolerance towards other individuals and the social position that he holds. The leader chooses his own space and the follower

It is only by creating the conditions in which the horse cannot avoid confronting us that we can initially hope to interact with him.

leaves that space and takes whatever remains, always remaining part of the herd but with fewer rights.

Let's imagine the scenario in which we belong to a herd and, as an individual, we are minding our own business grazing, and a subject who is a grade below us in the hierarchy starts to come near. We can decide to tolerate him; we can even be happy to have some company and happily nibble away together at close quarters, comforted by a sense of belonging. How nice! Now imagine that, after a while, we notice that about ten metres away from us there is some grass that looks particularly delicious and that post is occupied by a member who belongs to a higher social class than ours. Well, we can't simply go over there and suddenly invade his space, because we would be expelled forcefully and decisively and the more decisive our action to go over there, the more decisive the reaction will be of the other individual to reject us. Knowing that (having been educated to it), we will try to get closer, but always keeping an eye on the attitude of the horse whose space we intend to invade, and at the first sign of intolerance, if we don't want to incur his most dire wrath, we should be ready to change course.

Therefore we proceed … but what are the signs that we should be reading? Let us remember that we are entering into someone else's house and we need to use tact to understand whether or not we are welcome.

If the attitude doesn't change – that is, the individual doesn't change his state, it's a good sign and it means that, up until now, we are being tolerated and therefore if nothing happens we can proceed without much difficulty. If, on the other hand, perceiving our attempt to get near, he stops chewing, his eye tends to change shape or his ears move, it would be better for us to give up without invading his living space. If we were to continue we would certainly be violently attacked, but we wouldn't do so because the signals sent to us are more than sufficient for us to understand that, at least in that moment, our presence within his space will not be tolerated. All of this is communicated without rash signals, but just subdued and continuous ones. In fact, the horse hasn't even raised his head and hasn't attacked us, but would certainly have done so if we had continued in our intent.

Now, the thing to understand is that the signs described above are still too strong and exceed normal parameters, which are even less evident, except in cases of educating the

FEEL course instructor Maria Francesca Patrizi.

young who, as we know, tend, through natural exuberance, to challenge the tolerance of the herd who will educate them.

So the variation of space brings contact, and the first contact is obtained through the variation of space.

This conclusion could appear incorrect where eye contact is concerned since it can take place from a long distance, but if we look at this from another point of view, where contact is interaction, we will understand better.

For example, we are sitting on a park bench, where just twenty metres away, people are continually passing by. We can watch them and vice versa, without necessarily having any interaction, but if one of these people changes direction and starts to walk towards us, we will start to take into consideration the possibility that he might want something from us and, the closer he comes to us, the more we prepare ourselves, quite involuntarily, for interaction. We begin to note other fundamental elements as the direction and the intention: we will meet them more later.

But there is more: *a leader dominates and manages his space and a follower belongs to it.*

It's as if we went camping and found a space to pitch our tent and feel at home. Therefore, in that moment, we consider that space as our property, even though only temporarily. If the owner asks us to move, it's not a problem; we take down our tent and re-pitch it a bit further on. It's not exactly like that, but it gives us a good idea.

The living space for a horse can vary according to his circumstances, state of mind and overall situation. Let's imagine a circle around him of about ten metres in diameter within which the horse feels at home, or rather *that space is his home.*

Our concept of home – a space surrounded by walls, within which we feel protected, is unthinkable to a horse who has always lived in open spaces. (The stable is a prison! It is not a living space … it is not protection!) In fact the horse takes his home with him wherever he goes; the walls are made of air rather than brick and its dimensions can vary.

In understanding this concept, we will also understand that to enter into someone else's house without being invited is not a good thing …. Our objective, of which we should never lose sight, is not that of coercing, without the possibility of choice, but to earn the horse's respect and trust.

(That said, to enclose the horse in a space of 'circumscribed' rather than constraining dimensions, large enough to give the him the option to move and make choices is, initially, the only way to establish a relationship with him since, otherwise, if he had the chance, he would simply avoid us by moving away. We cannot compete with him in a race.

It is only by creating the conditions in which the horse cannot avoid confronting us that we can initially hope to interact with him.

We need an enclosure.

It must be said that there are other strands of thought that foresee this in open spaces. They foresee a whole series of 'rituals' to interact. Certainly very beautiful and efficient, but in my opinion they need a very deep understanding of the being of the horse, and lots of time. In this book, by choice, I will not deal with these topics since I think that, at first, working in open spaces without an expert trainer can be very complex and de-motivating. Although it is a journey I would recommend to anyone who already has good experience of interaction with horses, as this will open the horizons and lead to complementary journeys. The important thing for now, is to start to understand them and to start to interact.

So, after having placed our friend in a space which is preferably round and no smaller than twenty metres in diameter, we will start our observations without entering the enclosure, just to try to understand with whom we are dealing. We will try to understand who he is through

Working from the ground in wide open spaces without fencing.

what he does, how he does it and in what way he faces new things; if he is impulsive, frightened, scared, aggressive … and above all we give him time to become familiar with a new and confined space.

Let's allow him to explore and wait until his reactions become calmer and more reflective. Let's wait therefore, until he is aware and has acquired the knowledge that he cannot escape, cannot avoid remaining within certain spatial limits, but can, however, move and change his own status at his pleasure.

Usually I do not start any action until the horse has understood and accepted that he is in a bordered place with impassable boundaries.

This is already a lot for a wild-born animal! He has to accept a change of state, from freedom to incarceration, from 'I can if I want' to 'I can't even if I'd like to'. This, for him, is a great trial and it will take time until he begins to accept it.

Naturally, all of this has a different value for horses who are raised by humans, already accustomed to such parameters.

Once our friend has accepted the space, its limits and everything placed inside it, we can begin to enter into his home, into his domain.

CHAPTER 5

But What Do We Want From Him?

We want to ride him, we want a friend to share thousands of adventures with, to canter in boundless meadows, to take part in sporting competitions and excel at everything, jump ditches, cross rivers ….

Now, if I were a horse, I would tell you to get lost …. Don't even think about it. You want what? Mount on my back? You just try to get near me and I'll strike you down.

To him, all that we want is not what he wants. He doesn't want it and he doesn't want it. Have I already said he doesn't want it?

But this is not important to us, because it's what we want. And we will do anything to get it.

Why?

Because it makes us feel good, because we need to feel that somehow he belongs to us and becomes part of our world, of our way of seeing things and our way of living. Do you see what we expect of him?

And in exchange for what?

Unrequested affection, unwanted interaction, a relationship which he would readily do without.

Our needs in exchange for his freedom. It's no small thing we are asking!

Of course we will take care of him, but at what price? Who would nowadays, be willing to give up their freedom in exchange for board, lodging and medical care?

We expect affection from our horse that he would readily do without. Our needs in exchange for his freedom. It's no small thing!

I have never seen equitation as a competitive sport; it isn't and never will be, in that there is nothing sporting in depriving another living being of its freedom, just to get results to please oneself, where a 'good horse' is so judged only on physical grounds, related to competition. Just as the trade in coercive tools (like 10,000 different types of bit that can inflict varying degrees of pain), kills the relationship and skill of communication, so competitions can kill the good feeling of the relationship with the horse, by focusing only on the result.

But do we really need competition?

Apparently, yes. Our need to possess and to excel is part of our nature and our evolution, but, I believe, we could do it with a different sensitivity. Philippe Karl has battled and is battling to try to change some of the rules of dressage, which really go against any criteria of common sense but which are so deeply rooted in the socio-political culture and have been for so long, that even the evidence of what is obvious seems unable to change them. This is unnatural in that it is deprived of adaptability and so static as to be dangerous – but still it doesn't change.

However, we can cheer our gloomy thoughts, redirecting them to where each of us can make small changes that will contribute to the improvement of the interaction between human and horse, and so, for now leaving aside often sterile controversy, let's turn our minds back towards our horses.

The first thing to achieve, for our security and for harmony, is respect. This is fundamental and without this, communication would not be possible in that it would be ignored and trampled on. But how does one get it? And, above all, how does one give it? Firstly we have to understand that everything is an 'illusion' and is based on the horse considering tangible something that is really ephemeral. We must make him believe that we have control over him.

There are some things, at least in this first phase, which play to our advantage.

The first is that we are potential predators. He knows this and therefore normally fears us. Although a tiger is not bigger than a horse, it can bring him down. Horses are instinctively aware of such matters and it is to our advantage that the horse, like most prey animals, through empirical experience, doesn't determine a predator in terms of size but in terms of aggressiveness, and we are potential predators.

So let's concentrate and be careful not to reveal our tricks and, above all, don't let him understand that he could squash us like an ant.

We should always remember that we are dealing with an animal who, even though gentle, has significant mass and power, a set of formidable muscles, and that safety, first ours and then consequently his, should always come first.

Let's take a look at our equipment and compare it with theirs. We are equipped with:

- Poor speed
- Little physical strength
- No fangs or claws
- Huge intelligence (moot point!)

while they have:

- Great speed
- Great physical strength
- Long levers that can be used as weapons
- Intelligence that cannot be compared to that of man.

At least in one way – intelligence – we are superior, but only in that one; we have nothing else to use in our defence in a confrontation, so we should use it to the best of our abilities, primarily to avoid conflict. It is not necessary, and we should equally avoid developing tools of coercion, in order to obtain what we want (which we will not, in any case, get) and instead try to understand how these mysterious beings, in nature prey animals, work and develop a useful language with which to interact with them. Then, we will achieve more in less time and with more safety and harmony.

This absolutely does not mean to say, that our relationship with the horse should be that of prey and predator – absolutely not. We could not achieve trust and collaboration if we were to base our relationship on this. What is explained above is purely in order that we understand that, initially, this protects us from the mass of the horse, inasmuch as he fears us, but things will have to change.

CHAPTER 6

Who Am I? But, More Importantly, Who Are You?

When I start to interact with a horse, I first try to understand his character. Is he curious, suspicious, tolerant …? I make a first assumption, based on observing him at liberty and then, on this hypothesis, I start to build a work plan with him, either confirming such initial hypothesis, or changing it all completely, depending on his behaviour, which will reveal itself as the work progresses.

The important thing is not to fix ourselves on an initial idea; we have to be ready to change, adapting to it, without prejudice.

Let's suppose that we have entered the ring and that we find ourselves at the centre of it while our friend, on the other hand, is standing nice and quiet at the furthest point, not even gracing us with a look – in fact, turning his attention to the outside, as if we didn't exist or simply because something more interesting is happening out there.

What does he make of us?

I don't know, but definitely not something to interact with and even less as his leader. This is no good.

Things have to change

You will have no doubt noticed what happens, for example, when two horses who do not know each other and who are never normally together are put outside in the open: they approach each other, they sniff each other and after that, one of the two subjects 'imposes' on the other to go away, to back off, to concede space, more or less depending on the level of aggression. Time lapsed? A few seconds and the hierarchy is established.

If we carefully analyse what has happened, in order to understand the two horses, we will need to comprehend how the dominant one places himself in respect of the dominated one so as to reproduce his intent. To simply imitate their physical attitudes without a deep conviction of the act is completely useless, and, especially when we are dealing with an aggressive individual, it can be dangerous, but we will deal with this particular matter later. Don't even think about 'educational punishment': it does not exist. Only the conditions of dominating or being dominated exist and we should always remember that, to dominate, all we need to do is to make the horse move a bit. We must have the knowledge of the attitudes of the dominated, without which we would not have the basis on which to carry out our actions.

Let's see their respective attitudes. The dominant horse has:

- Ears pulled backwards
- Mouth open with teeth protruding with the intent to bite and charge
- A tail that swishes restlessly
- A back end that turns ready to kick

Whereas the dominated horse:

- Yields to pressure, conceding space
- Tends to follow the dominant subject, paying him attention

Clearly this is a simple and incomplete description, which is intended to allow us to recognize potentially dangerous attitudes (safety first). To succeed in understanding the real motivations behind these attitudes is, and will always be, the objective of reciprocal understanding. Often, aggressive attitudes can hide fear or uncertainty, anxiety and so on and only with time, without excluding anything *a priori* will we be able to accustom ourselves to that particular horse and consequently assume the appropriate attitudes with him. We don't need to be psychoanalysts; it will suffice, as always, to show sane common sense.

Attentive, interested

Relaxed

Sleepy, indisposed, submissive   Angry and aggressive

One day, a dear friend told me the difference between dominance and authority, explaining that dominance is obtained through submission whereas authority derives from recognition of what we are and what we do. It is clear then that we cannot, in any way, oblige a horse to accept our authority and that, for this to happen, we need to earn this acceptance.

A horse is a herd animal and will therefore willingly accept to be led provided that he recognizes in us the characteristics required of a leader.

Theirs is not blind faith and the fact that the horse obeys us is not a consequence of collaboration. Obedience can be induced by submission, but collaboration can only be achieved by obtaining their esteem and respect. Only thus can our authority be recognized.

I would need another book to deal only with this topic, which is so rich in fascinating nuances, but my hope resides in the fact that, with time and practice, readers can find the best path towards establishing at least a balanced rapport with their horses. One can give guidelines,

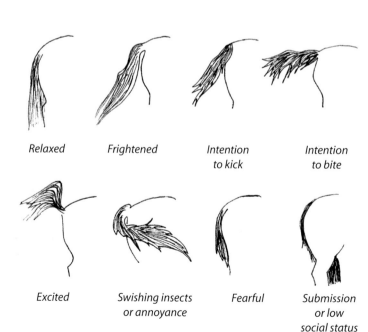

Relaxed   Frightened   Intention to kick   Intention to bite

Excited   Swishing insects or annoyance   Fearful   Submission or low social status

but their direct application will nonetheless have to be personalized. Clearly, personalizing does not mean adapting a form of communication to one-self, but rather mastering it to the point of feeling it one's own way and adapting the expressive requirements to the numerous variables, which we will inevitably encounter in interacting with horses. The ability to shape communication and adapt it to the common requirements in an attempt to create a rapport which is firmly based on reciprocal collaboration can only come with time. Experience is, in

1 Frightened, alert   2 Aggressive attitude
3 Attack   4 Fighting

many cases, a teacher who cannot be replaced. A correct study, and a suitable practice carried out under the guidance of a good teacher, are only meant to shorten the learning curve, which will also be determined by personal ability, but there are no short-cuts. The risk of being misunderstood is part of the game, but I would ask only one thing of anyone trying to benefit from the hints which this book can offer: 'always use common sense' in both your interests and the horse's. Excessive aggression as an end in itself is never a good path to follow; it can only make sense if it is used to re-establish the parameters of safety, harmony and lightness.

To be able to initiate any interaction, we need to get the horse's attention. How do we do this?

THE WHAT AND THE HOW

The 'what to do' depends strictly on the horse's reactions, whilst the 'how to do it' follows strict guidelines.

Hence, the 'what to do' (that is, make him go forward, change direction and gait, as well as the intensity and number of our requests) depends directly on the reactions of the horse, on how he learns, on his character, on the environment and so on and must necessarily be interpreted on the spur of the moment. The 'how to do it', on the other hand, will fortunately be subject to rules that have been clearly drawn up and established by the grammatical structure of the language.

Therefore, observing a horse's reactions will determine our actions. The intensity of the pressure will be linked to these same reactions, and to know how to judge the correct reactions will be the parameter we will always have to follow.

We will have to judge and act. Awareness and justice; awareness in judging and acting without delay in the most appropriate way, that which is just.

We have said that the 'what to do' can be chosen, whilst the 'how to do' follows rigid rules to which we must adhere. Let's say then that we want to send the horse forwards.

It doesn't matter at the moment in which gait, but let's just tell him that he has to go away from the place where he is, moving himself forwards.

The 'what' is resolved, now let's see how.

When we ask something, we apply a pressure, therefore from now on, request or pressure will be the same thing.

The pressure that we apply is not, in this context, manifest in physical contact, but rather to the horse's reaction, with which he manifests his acknowledgement of the same. Confirmation of the correct response, or anyway of a response in line with the request, should be given by the immediate interruption, or clear lessening, of the request or pressure (descent of aids).

The repetition and interruption of the request and therefore of the pressure in one or more given situations, where these criteria correspond to a given response or gesture by the horse, will be interpreted by him as a response to the pressure because the pressure ceases at the very moment of the positive reaction (response). The consequential logic of all this is an association – that is to say that a particular response becomes 'associated' with that particular request.

We are teaching. And he who teaches, learns.

And this is the concept of the 'comfort zone' and the 'discomfort zone', where the zone must be understood both in a physical and abstract manner; that is, in an abstract manner as the learning of a concept not linked to place, and in a physical manner as a place linked to the concept.

Let's try to understand this better.

If we want to teach the horse to do a lateral flexion of the neck (clearly at our request, since he has been capable of doing it on his own since birth), we should apply pressure until the horse starts to yield and flexes in the requested direction. Therefore 'pressure-reply-yield' and the resulting attainment of comfort. In this case, we have sought a certain movement in line with our request, not by a conditioned association but through a link between a 'comfortable zone' and a place.

We will now talk about an 'uncomfortable zone', linked instead to a physical place. For example, in the ring, the horse runs off to a certain zone – who knows, maybe because there is a tractor parked nearby and he darts off, increasing his speed at each step until he finally adopts a more serene attitude when he gets away from it.

So by the tractor is the discomfort zone; away from the tractor is the comfort zone. This, at least, until we decide to intervene and invert things, applying pressure to the horse in his comfort zone (where he seeks to relax), and taking it away as soon as the horse enters his discomfort zone.

He will thus find himself in a stalemate situation: between a discomfort caused by the tractor but without real danger and a discomfort zone caused by us. If we do not yield, he will be forced to change his parameters for getting out of a difficult situation. As he deals with the problem and understands that there is no real danger, that will become his comfort zone, where he will tend to slow down until he stops, which we, of course, will more than willingly allow. The physical comfort zone.

The concept is always the same, and always will be. The structure of the language does not change; the intent does.

To enable us to approach teaching, we need another fundamental element ... do you remember the nightmare of Captain Hook?

Tick tock, tick tock, tick tock.

CHAPTER 7

Timing

Timing is the other element of primary importance and is itself a fundamental part of the structure of the language.

In fact, we could say that up until now we have managed to learn all the notes and to read them in the score, but that if we tried to play them, only confused sounds would emerge. We know how to distinguish a 'do' from a 'fa', but we don't know their value, their duration, their accent. A rhythm is needed; the right timing. This element that seems so easy to understand will prove to be the most absolutely difficult to execute. Two different songs can be composed with the same identical notes, but with different timing and rhythm. The timing makes the difference. Anyone who has studied music or who delights in playing a musical instrument knows perfectly well what I am talking about.

To know how to play an instrument or sing is none other than the ability to manage to release specific sounds at specific times. To all effects it is a language; just not a conventional one. Now the problem is that everyone can appreciate a beautiful song, but understanding its structure and then faithfully reproducing it is quite another thing. Only, this is the very thing that we have to do and our instrument has a 'soul' and a life of its own. It's a bit like wanting to play a piano (assuming that we were able to), that canters, kicks, bites, trots, changes direction suddenly ….

To apply pressure at the wrong moment, and especially to interrupt it at the wrong moment, too soon or too late, completely upsets the interpretation of our request. In speaking of too soon or too late in terms of time, we mean instants or fractions of a second. This is the margin within which we can communicate with horses in a correct and satisfying manner.

When playing the piano and when riding a horse, a rhythm and the right timing are needed.

An *instant*, in the context of communication between human and horse, should be understood as that 'moment' in which the horse has the correct reaction to the request, which must, in that very same instant, be stopped or diminished.

Hence it should be said that the request must be stopped, or at least diminished, in the moment in which the horse 'means' to execute it or is predisposed to do it – that is, an instant before he actually executes it. In 'learning', which is different from gymnastics or from training, one needs to reward the intention of doing, in order to increase the response and the action and to always keep the horse's mind ready and reactive. Here we have introduced, in order to take it much further, the fundamental concept of intention.

There is in fact a huge difference between learning and gymnastics.

'Just as the learning phase awakens the attention of the horse through the attraction of novelty, so the repetitive character of training brings boredom and distraction.'

PHILIPPE KARL

It is vital to be able to recognize the yielding of a horse with precision and to give it the correct interpretation. Every time we apply pressure to the horse, putting him in an uncomfortable situation, be sure that he will try to get out of it, using a change in state. This is positive; it's what we want. The horse's attempts to re-attain a 'comfortable' situation will also certainly include the very action we want to steer him towards. It is now up to us to recognize it and to send the horse a positive signal (interrupt pressure; yield) that he can associate with that movement or action that he has made.

When time is of the essence, it can be our best ally or worst enemy.

If not interrupted at the right moment, our pressure can go on to interact with the next action (one that we don't want) and confirm that one instead, and so on, aligning a series of confirmations to actions we don't want and causing chaos in communication. The system goes into tilt. With the world 'timeliness', we must never think of frenetic actions.

The horse will do what we don't want him to do: that which we have unwittingly requested and moreover confirmed that he should do, all because of wrong timing. We cannot speak 'more slowly' in order to make him understand better. This concept does not exist in horses' language. Only constant repetition itself will confirm that certain action. Naturally, the same thing will happen if we release the pressure too soon.

Consistency is the only possible solution, and timing defines its correctness. A good teacher is one who teaches much to many in a simple way. We also have to note well that the sequence of pressure-yielding is never an on-off sequence, but a fluid one with a communicative continuity.

Therefore, let's not fumble about, but build as clear as possible a mental image of the action that we want to ask for. Then, with the certainty of having the horse's attention and the awareness that he is perfectly capable of executing what we are about to ask, we will start to give the correct pressure, awaiting his reaction which we will confirm once he has carried it out, putting the horse once again in a comfortable condition. (Comfortable condition based on the contact and not on the loss of it.)

By pressure or uncomfortable condition, I never mean the creation of a situation of stress, in that stress will block the learning process, favouring instead the occurrence of a behaviour of self-defence stemming from survival instincts.

Therefore, in layman's terms 'give comfort to positive responses and maintain a situation of discomfort to negative responses'.

Let's close the first circle.

The efficiency and the reason why this system works is always to be found in and brought back to the *primary need:* energy.

If we have really understood this concept, we will be able to close the circle and therefore to always find a logical and coherent response to our request. The correct use of the concept of comfort and discomfort will go on to create the motivation engendered by this primary need.

A motivated horse will collaborate; a constrained horse will defend himself.

The first request must always be made at the lowest level of possibilities, that is to say a little, slowly, gently, smoothly and lightly and must be interrupted or lessened immediately at the first sign of a positive reaction, reverting then to contact, with which everything starts and finishes.

CHAPTER 8

Grammatical Concepts

Taking, for example, the horse in liberty, we need to take into account two elements: our position in respect of the horse and the direction in which we direct our pressures.

In stable conditions of the horse, we must maintain a neutral position, which is usually directly behind the horse's shoulder.

This is a position of stability and contact, inasmuch as it is logically found in a neutral zone. Even from a geometrical point of view it is found in the middle of the horse, as measured from the attachment of the tail, to the tip of the nose when the horse is relaxed. This is important in that we can apply pressure either towards the front part, to slow, stop, change direction and so on, or towards the rear part, to ask him to go forwards and to increase the gait.

Neutral zone.

If our objective is that of having a horse who has self-carriage, pressure should not be kept up in a constant manner, otherwise we risk desensitization, unresponsiveness and heaviness in the horse.

We must teach the horse to execute our request. We mustn't do it for him; we mustn't physically participate in doing it, but instead we must make him do it, fighting our instinct to help him in a physical manner, simply because we can't.

We can, however, prepare him and put him in the best condition to be able to comply and, as a consequence, be able to execute a certain exercise.

If we respect our role, he will respect his.

The horse has no need of support; support is a defence to which we drive him, as is instability; unstable horses do not exist in that all horses tend towards stability, simply because it involves less expenditure of energy and is much more pleasurable. We always need to remember that the horse can lessen his response to requests, both those made from the ground or from the saddle.

Requests must *never* be continuous but must be increased, even brusquely (aggression), in case of little or no reaction and must be stopped or noticeably lessened, as soon as a positive reaction is obtained.

Note how when moving from the neutral position (photo 1) to the active position (photo 2) with a small movement of the shoulders, the horse looks at us and perceives our variation of state preparing himself to execute our requests. The accentuated movement of my shoulders in photos 3 and 4 serve only to better allow the reader to understand the action. The important thing to understand is that the horse would not have required this. Sensing that we have been understood and interrupting our request in that movement will keep the horse vigilant and attentive. Everything we do that goes beyond this limit of perception will desensitize the language, rendering communication excessive and therefore heavy.

Therefore the grammar will be:

- Neutral contact or position
- Request
- Reaction (on the part of the horse)
- Interruption of the request
- Neutral contact or position

The only cases in which pressure should be maintained are when it is opposed, or in over-sensitive horses in order to desensitize them, in an attempt to establish a 'normal reactivity'. Nevertheless, it must be interrupted at the first sign of a positive reaction which, in the latter case, will be non-reaction to certain disturbing actions.

An example of this latter case is shown in the photo sequence.

CHAPTER 9

Desensitization

To understand how to use the method of desensitization to an external stimulus, let's suppose that we are dealing with a hypersensitive or badly educated subject, who, on the lunge rein or in the ring, tends to escape suddenly every time we make a certain action – let's say every time that we clap our hands (external stimulus). In this case our instinct would be to interrupt that action in order to quieten the horse down. But if we do this and if, moreover, we repeat this over time, we are doing nothing other than reinforcing the horse's conviction that every time he escapes we will interrupt our action, putting him in a comfortable situation which, by association, he will repeatedly seek at every recurrence of these conditions. We will therefore achieve the opposite effect.

Instead, we must repeat our action until the horse begins to calm himself down. It doesn't matter how long it takes for this to happen. We must persevere and it will happen, because he will eventually see that to escape won't bring him to a state of comfort, but will produce only tiredness and waste of energy, in that the disturbance we are creating will continue until his state changes, rather than ours.

Then yes, things will change, in that the association produced will, in time, lead him to more reasoned and less compulsive reactions.

What I have said so far on desensitization needs a clarification: most situations that include excessive reactions by the horse usually include a mistaken action on our part, through inexperience or lack of understanding of the horse's attitude. As I have said before, a horse cannot be false by nature: therefore, if he is placed in uncertain conditions which result in defensive reactions, he will always communicate this to us but, because of our own limitations, we simply don't pick up on this attitude hence desensitization often serves to correct our mistakes.

To clarify this concept better, here is an example: horse versus crackly plastic bag. We are in the centre of the ring with a crackly bag in our hand and the horse is at the furthest part of the perimeter observing us with curiosity and some concern over this novelty (the crackly bag). By carefully observing the reactions of the horse and assuming (in reality it might be different) that he has accepted the fact that we have a bag in our hand, with relative calm we very slowly start to move the bag repeatedly in a slow crescendo. If the horse runs off, we have made a mistake.

Why? Because we have not read the horse's reactions well and we have not interrupted our action a moment before it has become intolerable to him (too much pressure).

Surely the horse demonstrated his discomfort at the increase of our disturbing action and, if we had interrupted it at the opportune moment, we would have given him the opportunity to reflect and to return to a calm condition, so we could then repeat it again, to arrive at his limit, then interrupting and repeating it, but never going over the limits of pressure imposed by his reactions.

Horse vs. crackly plastic bag.

In this way, repeating and interrupting our actions with the correct timing, the horse will increase his tolerance to the potential danger we are creating and this would be perfect execution, which requires, on our part, great tact, patience, experience and self-assuredness.

That ideal scenario would be wonderful, but we make mistakes; the horse will escape, our timing will not be right and this will teach us that we have pushed that horse too far. It doesn't matter – nothing has been wasted – our experience grows and our extraordinary human nature shows us once again how to learn from our mistakes.

What is important is to keep an open mind, putting ourselves in the condition to understand, interpret and translate the equine language made up of attitudes; attitudes which not only belong to their world but also to ours, to a world of which we have been an integral part in a journey made of changes, where our evolutionary speed often does not coincide with theirs.

They cannot accelerate, but we can and must slow down a bit to be able to rediscover that part of us which is more in symbiosis with their way of expressing themselves.

It is clear that, in the moment the horse escapes, we must not interrupt our action but must continue to wave the bag, trying always to maintain the same intensity and action until the horse, owing to the increase of self-inflicted uncomfortable conditions (tiredness and energy consumption), induced but not requested by us, can no longer bear them and will, therefore, have to change them whether he wants to or not.

To achieve this, it is sometimes necessary to push the horse to his physical limits, so that exertion, which produces exponentially unpleasant sensations and is especially unsustainable over time, may bring him to develop reasoning and to find the solution to a stalemate situation. As the proverb goes: 'fatigue is the mother of invention'.

For this reason, the dimensions, the ground and the fencing in which we execute these actions are of fundamental importance. A ring that is too small, or ground that is not suitable, can cause a lot of damage to the horse's health, as can inadequate fencing, which can cause the horse to think he can jump it.

Let's delve for a second into the subject of fatigue; it is worth doing since it will help us understand horses a bit better. Further on we will meet another variable that will be useful to modify the mental process of horses, for example the escape: that is, their curiosity.

In the society in which we live today it is really difficult for us to rationally understand the attitudes of the horse, in that it inevitably takes us through an evolution of thought which is very different from that which we would have had living in different times, even if the objective is the same.

It almost seems that our empirical heritage can't catch up with our intentions, which are always attracted by what is to come, rather than what has passed.

I simply want to say that mechanisms that trigger our reasoning and our thoughts have changed in their substance as a consequence of the changing of our needs. And this is precisely the point – what are our needs?

Education, a good job, a family, affection: I could make a very long list before arriving at survival pure and simple. All of our thoughts are now aimed at how to better our life, taking it for granted, within certain limits imposed by time.

Our natural predators are illnesses and accidents. Ferocious beasts, bad weather and lack of food no longer belong to our society and consequently no longer form part of our concerns, which no longer influence our way of acting and thinking. Science and technology have virtually eliminated the fear of danger and of the unknown from our existence.

Curiosity is our primary resource. It allows us to learn, no longer being limited by fear, and it is its decrease that has led us to a radical change in being and in acting.

Fear is inversely proportional to curiosity and curiosity is the spring that triggers evolution in the form of learning growth.

What we take for granted, horses don't. Our survival instinct has changed; theirs hasn't. We know that we can go and calmly take a walk in the woods without meeting packs of wolves or worse; we know that they aren't there, but since when? Two hundred, three hundred, five hundred years? One thousand years? And what are these spans in evolutionary terms? Nothing, if we think of a process between prey and predator that has always been there. The horse fears what he doesn't understand and seeks to give it as much distance as possible. We are made curious by it and are therefore attracted to it.

He is a prey animal, always ready to trigger his defence mechanism in the face of what he doesn't understand or know, and a horse who defends himself, even when he doesn't defend himself against us, is potentially dangerous in that fear produces loss of control caused by the triggering of his instinctive survival mechanisms, such as uncontrolled flight which, if we are in the saddle, is not pleasant, especially in open spaces.

For this reason it is important to understand the mental processes of the horse and to find a way of keeping them under more control, trying to add new elements to their way of acting.

One of these fundamental elements is that *escaping serves no purpose*. We have to manage to teach the horse that escaping serves no purpose and that our proximity, viewed as belonging to the herd, means safety, and the bigger the danger the more the herd draws together. Then, especially if the leader is calm, there is no reason to be concerned. We have to win their trust.

But nature is often obstinate, especially when there is no understanding, and flight is the first and most important weapon at the horse's disposal. It is not easy to explain to him that it is no longer necessary.

We can't make a horse understand *what a tractor is*, but we can make him understand that it is not a potential danger for him.

Learning is strenuous, especially if the brain is not particularly conditioned to carry out such tasks. Therefore, if we allow the horse to make the choice between understanding and escaping, the latter will always be the obvious choice; the one that is more a part of him.

Only if we manage to interact with the horse in an efficient way can we hope to be able to change some of the attitudes that are natural to him and dangerous to us, and exertion is often the key to comprehension; an indispensable instrument with which we can try to change some attitudes and begin to develop a different mental process, using elements of trust capable of developing and reinforcing in the horse a sense that we belong, to the point where we can be taken as a behavioural example.

We are in an evolutionary phase that differs from that of the horse and we must not forget this. Hence we will no longer wonder why the horse escapes in front of an innocuous plastic bag. It's what he sees and especially how he sees it that counts, not what we see. Is it right that we try to change him? I don't know for certain, but I know that it is right to increase the horse's and our safety and, to be able to do this, we must be the first ones to change in the name of an undesired partnership, at least on the part of the horse. We have created a world to cater for mankind, and everyone and everything else has to adapt to it. The greater the level of interaction, the more radical the requested change has to be. It is true that, in the wild, a horse hardly exceeds twelve years of age, (as do many horses used in equestrian sport in Europe – 2003 FEI statistical investigation – a statistic that should at least make us think about what we ask of them for our personal glory), whereas horses in captivity can easily reach thirty years or more. But they don't know this and we can't put this in front of them as a reasoned choice of lifestyle. What we can do is make their conditions

Maria Francesca Patrizi with Festosa (FEEL Course).

better when we want to interact with them … and to *understand them* is the first thing to do.

Many people approach horses without having the slightest idea of what a horse is. This is normal; the problem is that they then continue to do so. To err is human, but to persevere is diabolical.

Going further into the topic of desensitization, we must distinguish two principal phases and two different methods of action: to understand whether a horse flees as a result of FEAR, or MOVES AWAY out of prudence. To understand these attitudes in constrained spaces is not simple since, in nature, if a horse flees out of fear the flight can go on for kilometres whereas, if he is moving away out of prudence, he will only do so for a maximum of thirty to forty metres. In this respect also, experience and common sense will indicate the right interpretation. Flight is absolute and determined; moving away, on the other hand, has the principal characteristic of quickly losing intensity even if, in the first few metres, it can resemble flight. Hence, if we recognize that our horse is not fleeing but moving away out of prudence, the best way of proceeding is to stimulate his curiosity. The horse himself suggests this; he feels that something is not clear, but the fact that we remain calm induces him to 'reflect': 'Is this a good thing or a bad thing?' He offers us the benefit of doubt, and not to take advantage of this would be stupid, if nothing else. In nature, prey cannot afford to be too curious, but today, with us, the horse can and, if we teach horses to be curious when they are with us, we will work with the pleasure rather than with the effort of discovery. By sensitizing the horse to the innocuous nature of the plastic bag, starting by massages with the bag closed in our hand, and slowly opening it, there will be no effort, just interest. In just a few minutes we will be able to place the plastic bag between his ears. Or we can do pleasant things together next to the tractor, even placing an apple on the seat for him to take, first with the motor stopped and then with it running, and so on. We are always faced with the enigma of correct comprehension which, if well interpreted, will result in sensible behaviour during education. Working on curiosity is satisfying for both parties. The mental processes that are activated are completely different from those induced by effort. Therefore, whenever we can, we should always prefer this type of teaching, even out of mere opportunism, since it is faster, longer-lasting, more efficient, non-stressful and stimulating …. And naturally this goes for both quadrupeds and non-quadrupeds. This stimulates the sense of collaboration, trust and belonging, which will increase with the number of positive experiences: 'tractor=apple' or 'plastic bag=little massage' that's 'nice, really nice!'. Horses are far from stupid! To say that we are the first to be educated is the usual platitude, but the life of a horseman is made of surprising platitudes. I adore platitudes; they are always so out of the ordinary!

So, effort is of no use? Rarely will it be useful. Sometimes it will be indispensable. Most of the time, we will need educational understanding and intelligence. Nothing is a foregone conclusion.

We must try as soon as possible to divide what happens daily with the work of the horse into two different types of situation: NEGATIVE and POSITIVE.

CHAPTER 10

Opposition

As we have done up until now, we will first look at this from the emotive-physical point of view, trying to understand it, then move on to finding the solutions in terms of the appropriate language and techniques to apply.

This will be our method of study and we will try to apply it for every single element. It is tedious but efficient and, as our understanding of the horse increases, so should our need to analyse things profoundly decrease.

There are various types of opposition that don't have a common root, but derive principally from problems of understanding and incorrect requests in terms of the level of preparation of the horse.

The first group includes those related to the lack of willingness, interest and pleasure and therefore non-collaboration on the part of the horse, and the second group include those that derive from requests for exercises that are often not yet within the reach of the horse – in other words which he is not yet able to do.

In both these cases, we are not dealing with deficiencies of the horse, but rather with gross errors on our part during the education process, and the techniques discussed are necessary to recover and remedy our failings.

We do not want to be in the unhappy position of pandering to his will without interfering too much for fear of triggering potentially dangerous reactions.

Now, taking for granted that a horse rarely puts up opposition if the educational procedure has been carried out in an appropriate manner, we shall analyse the first group.

OPPOSITION TO DOMINATION

We must never place the horse in conditions where he thinks he can fight us for leadership. This option must never exist, must never be included in the sphere of possibilities. The instinct to subjugate, stand above, repress – this is the domination I am speaking about and it must not be tolerated.

The problem that often, for varied reasons also derived from our unsatisfactory past experiences, it may be difficult to maintain dominance over him, and the moment he becomes aware of this, especially if he has a dominant character, we find ourselves going through some pretty bad moments, in the unhappy condition of pandering to his will without interfering too much for fear of triggering potentially dangerous reactions. In this situation, we are the ones who offer our collaboration and pander to his needs; we are followers, we have lost our dominant role, we depend on him. I, for one, absolutely do not want to depend on a mass of half a ton of muscle whose instincts often dominate his reasoning.

Loss of control is very dangerous, the rider knows when this happens; being perfectly aware of it … the problem is that so is the horse.

In this case both the horse and the rider are in need of re-education by an expert. The horse must again be submitted to the will of the rider and the will of the rider must once again return to an attitude of dominance.

Every time that I have come across these situations I have found that the dominance of the horse over the rider in the saddle was the result of a lack of control and therefore of a wrong attitude on the part of the rider, right from the preparation of the horse from the ground, and that this occurred in the first few moments of interaction. It is important how we act in front of the horse because our habitual gestures can induce him to assume a wrong attitude. For example, if a horse comes towards us whilst we are near him and we give him space by moving away, even a little bit, this can induce him to think that we are yielding space, which will consequently bring him to re-evaluate the roles and to revert from being dominated to being dominant. It is natural for us not to not make much of these simple things in that they are not immediately dangerous, but all it takes is one little step backwards.

We must never forget how and to what extent the language of the horse is based on physical attitudes and we don't only communicate with the horse when we are in the saddle, the ring, or while we are intent on 'doing' training. The concept of 'schooling' does not exist for the horse; either we are always the 'master' or we never are. We cannot turn horses off by turning a key; their interactivity is always connected with anyone within the compass of their interest and their assessment of behaviour or social status is always active and changeable. All of this is an integral part of their way of being. We, on the other hand, are losing this on our evolutionary journey, which has taken us towards a more verbal language, with more stable social conditions based on a much wider range of factors.

We tend to divide our lives into lots of sectors: school, work, family, friends, holidays and so on, and our behaviour varies depending on the sector we find ourselves in, as well as with whom we find ourselves. We can play a game of football against our boss and we will certainly not have the same behavioural attitude as when we are at work. In the horse's world, none of this exists. We must therefore be aware that, if we let him dominate, even unconsciously, while we saddle-up, clean his box, or other things, our role as a follower will not be redefined according to where we are or what work we are doing. The horse first evaluates with whom he is dealing; the location is a secondary association, even though it is very important.

If we become the follower, our decisions will become questionable and I don't think it's a good idea to table a discussion with a mass of muscle endowed with a very small brain, even though he is often wiser than us. We therefore need what my aviator friend Marcello Pichi Graziano calls a 'democratic dictatorship'.

A careful analysis of our actions will be necessary to re-establish social roles. If we are firm and coherent in our actions, the horse will have no other option but to adapt to them. Certainly, it will be a bit less romantic but far more sensible. Subsequently, if we want to, once we have re-established control, nothing can stop us making some concessions to the horse in the name of the huge love or affection that we feel for him, although always being aware of the limits beyond which we shouldn't venture.

We should not be frightened to change; the horse is endowed with social dynamism and will not take long to conform to and accept our changes.

Whilst re-educating horses, I have often witnessed, in a very evident way, their social awareness and how they are ready to change depending on who is interacting with them. In fact, during re-education, with me they would maintain proper behaviour and then change it suddenly with the owner. It is much easier to re-educate a horse than to get an owner to accept reality, even when faced by the most persuasive evidence.

The cure and the remedy often consist of back-tracking, looking at the horse for what he really is and trying to see things from his point of view. We must manage to see him and see ourselves through his eyes.

Not everyone can control the horse from the saddle; his defences at times can put us in serious difficulties and even those who can maintain control, prefer to avoid this. From the ground, things are different and most of us, with the right knowledge, are capable of doing a good job, reinforcing our own beliefs and consequently breaking the dominance of the horse. Once the preconceptions of the horse have been overcome and our role has been established through work on the ground it will be much easier to bring him to fulfil our will when we are in the saddle. Because the horse's will has become accustomed to complying with our demands, his possible oppositions will always be less convincing. The certainty of domination and of being dominant reinforce horses' beliefs, whilst the habit of following our requests and submitting to them makes them docile, putting them in a correct behavioural state, preparing the ground for the trust which will need to be won day by day.

Please note that these notions are to be applied to horses who show a real intention to subjugate us and therefore expose us to a real danger. Our primary objective will always be to create a relationship based on respect and collaboration.

I often tend to present these motivations as if they were obvious, and the difficulty in trying to describe the various situations could lead the reader to adopt excessively strong attitudes towards horses who are docile and misunderstood (a typology which embraces most horses). Clearly a 'sane' relationship will inevitably contain balances that are difficult to describe in all their variables …. The act of subjugating is not less incorrect than that of being subjugated but both, nonetheless, imply reactive consequences. These consequences must never affect our safety parameters. It is often too easy to maintain aggressive behaviour for too long and without the real need to do so. This is a situation that creates a false sense of security. A relationship based on fear never has pleasant outcomes. We must make a choice, and that choice, as the actor Totò would put it in his famous film, is to decide whether we are *uomini o caporali* (men or corporals).

DEFENSIVE OPPOSITION

These are those oppositions resulting from requests which are unsuitable for or non-compliant with the psychophysical state of the horse.

But what does that mean?

If we, for example, ask a youngster who has only just been backed to perform a piaffe, this request cannot be suitable, in that the horse will not be capable of executing it. Therefore, if we nonetheless decide to continue to insist on our request, we will obtain a reply that will not correspond to our request and the stronger our request the more inadequate the reply will be, thereby inducing a reactive or defensive opposition.

Certainly it's obvious that in these conditions no one would ask for a piaffe; to do so would be absurd. The problem is that, from the horse's point of view, we often ask equally absurd things. The goal that we are aiming to achieve should always be continuously assessed and we should be ready to change it to suit the psychophysical state of the horse; it is a case of 'we shouldn't ever ask what we are not able to achieve'. But, as I have already said, neither horses nor we are perfect and, as a consequence, mistakes – whatever they may be – will often accompany us on our journey.

The knowledge of techniques that allow us to correct our misdoings is of fundamental importance, provided always that we are able to recognize them.

In fact, it is often not easy to assess what we are able to achieve: to understand whether a horse won't do something because he is unable to. Then there is also the case of the horse 'doing' less than he could do …. In short, the subtleties are really many and complex and, in

The goal that we are aiming to achieve should always be reassessed continuously.

these cases, more than ever, we need certainty – certainty that can only derive from simple rules that will be our lifelines every time we set sail towards unknown destinations.

One of these lifelines is that, even if we make a mistake in executing a request, we must try to obtain a response as much in line with it as possible, without, at the same time, inducing excessive stress in the horse, which would trigger the mechanisms of self-defence.

Let's try to clarify this a bit with some examples.

Let's take the case where, for reasons yet unknown to us, one fine day, we wake up with the idea of teaching our horse 'travers' (haunches-in) and, after a bit of warming up, we ask him to walk and apply pressure with our outside leg, expecting as a logical consequence to feel his haunches move decidedly inwards. Very good, and once we have done that we go on to flying changes and incorporate some pirouettes, after which there is a familiar but annoying sound and we realize that it's time to get up and go to work. The dream is over; the alarm clock has gone off.

I'm not saying that this can't happen, indeed, it would be desirable, especially if we had worked hard before, but let's suppose that it does not happen and the horse is not, in his response, in line with our request, and let's consider the possibility of seeing different reactions.

Hypothesis: if, with pressure of our outside leg, what we achieve is that the horse's back tends to go out rather than in (hence the word opposition – to get an opposite and contrary reaction), what would our action be to his opposite reaction?

Let's see: if we interrupt our action (remove our leg) we will communicate to the horse that his reaction is correct in respect of our request, in that he is put in a comfortable situation by the interruption of the very request and, with time, he will associate this reaction with our action. No, that's no good. We mustn't interrupt the request; we must educate him and therefore explain to him that this is not what we want. If, whilst maintaining the request, the horse continues to give the wrong response, we must not lose sight of our objective and continue the request, keeping him in an uncomfortable situation that will induce him into changing his reaction. It may happen that the horse leans on our leg, tolerating it and becoming indifferent to it. In this case we should intensify the request and also use the schooling whip to help us, using it gently but with a growing intensity until we get a reaction. Even if it is not in line with our request it is always better than no reaction. We then interrupt the request with the schooling whip and continue the pressure with our leg until we get an adequate response, after which we immediately interrupt the pressure.

Another hypothesis is that, on the intensification of our request, the horse moves forward and tries to escape. In this case also we must not interrupt our request but must lessen it, trying to bring the horse back to walk whilst keeping our request active (*see* Chapter 13, Channelling Energy).

What we should not expect and wait for is a complete response before interrupting our request. Instead, what needs to be caught is 'the intention to do', 'the willingness to execute' and, as soon as the horse's response or reaction STARTS to be in line with our request, the same should immediately be interrupted, putting the horse in a comfortable situation, and we should gently stroke him.

Intention is the light of action.
SAINT AUGUSTINE OF HIPPO
Our Lord's Sermon on the Mount

(A pat on the neck can be tolerated, but it is definitely not liked. A slow and quiet stroke with gentle pressure is normally well accepted.)

By repeating these actions over time, we create the associations through which the horse is taught that, to that specific action (for example, that position of the leg), he must always respond with a specific reaction.

In other words, if travers (haunches-in) is our objective, initially we must interrupt our pressure as soon as the horse shows the intention to bring his haunches to the inside, even with a simple change of balance. Let's wait, give him time to create an association by repeating the action often and interspersing this exercise with 'efficient breaks' before asking him to do it for a lengthy amount of time. We must always be ready, even in more advanced phases, to return to execute exercises in brief and intense sessions, to increase his desire to respond as required every time we note a drop in his interest.

Exercises extended over long periods, especially on youngsters and therefore in the training stage, tend to make the horse indifferent and usually undermine his willingness and collaboration, which can also happen in gymnastic exercises, where it is often necessary to do them for long periods to increase efficiency.

CONSISTENCY AND INCONSISTENCY

What, for us, is a logical response to an action, for the horse is not. To educate the horse to provide the correct reaction makes the training coherent.

This, naturally, is only from our point of view. The study of technique, the development of the school of equitation, has led us over time to develop and confirm rules that we call universal, in that they are logical and consistent, as to how we assume and make the horse assume positions that assist the actions in the best way. Reflecting on this, it may be considered normal to conclude the correctness of the use of aids and of requests that should always be executed in a certain way and this way is, more or less, universally accepted.

In order to respect such 'rules' we often have to fight our instincts and the horse has to do the same.

We are derived from primates and the 'prehensile' instinct, for example, is deeply rooted within us. Consequently, using our hands for balance, grabbing at anything that comes our way, reins included, is one of our habits. If we decide not to do it, it is because, through education, we have learned the right reasons for this.

We cannot use the same logical procedure to teach the horse.

Thus we cannot make him understand that a certain reaction must correspond to a certain action in that it is logical, consequent and therefore coherent with it. Above all we should not expect it.

The horse is always coherent with his way of being and, as such, should at least be understood. So, if for us, learning is directly proportional to study and to its application, for the horse, learning must be understood as education in the coherence of the reactions.

This procedure requires trust in that it appears illogical and incoherent to the one being educated. In other words, we cannot explain to the horse why we want him to do a certain thing, in that he is not in the evolutionary condition to understand it. Understanding has therefore to be substituted by submission, which, if the method used is efficient, will go hand-in-hand with trust, transferring to us a sense of collaboration.

Let's hold on tight ... the sea's about to get rough!

We need reference points, safe moorings to which we can return every time navigation becomes too uncertain for us.

Fortunately, during our journey, we have concepts available to us that we can apply and which will help us to not get lost; but often finding the correct course can be an arduous task.

When I started studying to become qualified to fly and first began studying navigation, the concept that I had to immediately learn and understand was that of doing everything in my power to avoid trouble. For example, during a flight from point A to point B, we always had to have previously planned a point C or D in case B, for whatever reasons, was not reachable. Therefore, when my instructor asked me what I should do if, in attempting to reach my primary objective (let's say B), I encountered a big storm front, I proudly replied that I would have assessed whether to head towards C or D and that, if I noted clear skies at either, I would direct the plane there. His reply was 'Invert the bows and turn towards home – that is, put as much distance as possible between yourself and trouble.'

This immediately reminded me that this is also basically the same technique adopted by horses for millennia, and I honestly could not deny its effectiveness.

Now, the problem is that in attempting to educate horses, not only will we have to go and look for 'trouble' – we will also have to find alternative solutions to an (albeit dignified) flight.

To put the horse forward is one of these alternatives.

If we are trying to teach the horse shoulder-in and, to our amazement, we realize that, in reality, it looks more like a wrestling match than anything else and, even worse, one we are losing, then putting the horse forward, pretending that we really just wanted him to canter, is one of the best things to do. It will not teach the horse the shoulder-in; it will, however, give a response that will not create too many problems for us in the future, since to go forward is the solid base on which to build anything in equitation and which, above all, tends to prevent the manifestation of many of the horse's defences. Clearly, we must not make the horse canter every time we make a mistake, but it can help us in difficult situations we have created. Above all, once the horse has gone forward, we need to stroke him immediately, return to walk and calmly try not to repeat the chaos we have just left behind.

When we mount a youngster for the first time, a buck is natural – even if it is not to be tolerated – and, if it happens, the biggest mistake would always be to try to stop the horse or hold him back. In doing so we would put the horse in the best condition to intensify the action with an even higher arc. Managing instead to push him forward, even brusquely, we will have a much flatter arc, less harsh changes of direction, a more stable balance, and a greater consumption of energy, inducing exertion and therefore discomfort.

The figure of the authoritative educator is a difficult status to attain and just as difficult to maintain in time.

With experience we will learn to extricate ourselves from complicated situations without losing this status, but initially we will need to experiment, understand and learn with an open mind in order to be educated. We need patience and, paradoxically, often assuming the role of implacable judge with regard to our attitudes will be part of our method of acting. Patience in this case must be ambivalent, that is, applied to both horses and to ourselves. It is true that we are constantly being judged – or perhaps it would be better to say evaluated – but this is part of the evolutionary process of the horse.

Horses evaluate us in order to determine whether they can trust us. Right and wrong have different values in their evaluations. They are not interested in whether a particular exercise is correct or not. Their real interest always focuses more on 'how' than on 'what'. Our attitudes – how we behave with them in the act of educating – are what will be evaluated, not whether we succeed in making them execute a shoulder-in correctly. The study of the biomechanics of the type of horse will provide the correct parameters in which to carry out the appropriate exercise for the particular horse at the particular time. This will bring harmony to authority, which will nonetheless be attained through the 'how'. From the horse's point of view the difference is not subtle, but immense. The things that are fundamentally important to them will also need to become so to us. Only in this way can we ever hope to gain their trust. The horse's ability to adapt allows us to make mistakes and make up for them even after the lapse of time. Their preconceptions, assuming that they have them, are far less radical than ours. There are happy moments in every person's life, moments when that person has conscious intuitions of justified certainty, or at least so they believe. One of these moments, for me, is when what I feel becomes knowledge, and is repeated regularly each time I prepare a young horse. The feeling that, from that moment on, things will change radically is that moment of trust and an awareness that we depend on each other while maintaining distinct roles and identities. It is the awareness that we can trust one another and is the beginning of a real relationship based on mutual trust. When this happens, I don't think anyone can say other than that there is a sensation which quickly becomes concrete – tangible and unequivocal. We change together and together we trust. If we riders adopt too practical a point of view, one that is simply based on the achievement of the correct exercise, we forget that we are interacting with a living being and lose sight of the main objective, which consists in creating a correct procedure in the act of execution.

Let's not, therefore, persist in wanting to make the horse execute at all costs, but let's place our emphasis on preparing the horse and putting him in the best possible condition to execute.

CHAPTER 11

Interaction

Before trying to interact and therefore trying to control his movements, we must ask ourselves a serious question: 'what control do we have of ourselves?' Our success will depend on the answer we give. If we want to be efficient educators, we must have efficient control of our body and mind.

We manage to control our state and change it according to educational needs, suppressing, anger, rage, frustration, inconsistency, and so on. The list could be really long. We must be able to pass from a state of complete aggression to one of absolute calm in the space of a few moments, keeping a clear and open mind, assuming an attitude of educating and not one of punishing, repressing or obliging. Are we really ready to start an interaction with another being, who reasons and reacts in a different way, without being carried away by sentiments or states of mind which in some way could alter our knowledge and our objectives? If the reply is yes, by all means close the book and I can calmly tell you that you have wasted your money, you are already ready. Otherwise let's continue our journey and try to understand what lies ahead .... The first thing to do, before we become too involved, is to try to create an 'educational detachment', trying to see the horse as our pupil and never as our beloved little baby. It has been widely proved that if a surgeon knows his patient and has an intense or strong tie with him, the operation could be put at risk. Therefore let's not get too involved at an emotional level for both his and our sakes. A healthy distance that allows us to assess things clearly is the first condition necessary.

The second thing to do is to maintain this state at least during the educational phase.

I do not agree with current trains of thought that see the interaction between humans and horses always more immersed in the idea of humans identifying themselves as part of the herd itself. This implies his total detachment from human characteristics, with the intent of creating a 'real' collaboration based solely on trust and wholly following in the footsteps of nature. This, nonetheless, with the intent of jumping on his back. This seems hypocritical to me, since, in nature, I've never seen a horse carrying another one on his back. Of course I will be ready to withdraw this statement as soon as I do see it. It is one thing to study the language in order to understand and to be understood.

It is quite another to want to encourage people to turn themselves into horses in all respects. Therefore, every time that I have spoken, or will speak, of behaving like a leader or assuming the role of the head of the herd, I do not in any way mean that you should put yourself out to pasture with them and I assure you that there are those who do...

Clearly, to be able to understand them and therefore acquire an efficient bodily language, the more we manage to put ourselves in their shoes, the better, but this is quite another thing.

Criticism: 'Yes but then a horse will never see you as one of them' With any luck!

I wouldn't be happy if the stallion on duty measured himself up to me to see who had the right to mate. There is a limit beyond which we shouldn't venture. It is less natural, in my opinion, to assume the right that a horse should see us as a member of the herd, rather than as a human who wants to try to interact with him. Horses are collaborative also with other species, they meet through cohabitation and the emotive language, they collaborate if they cohabitate with dogs, cows, sheep…. And even with us. Adaptability is an extraordinary gift of the horse.

I will repeat it again at the risk of being boring. A horse is a horse and it is necessary that we see him for what he is for better or for worse. To accept that is, according to me, the best way to start to love him in as much as, perhaps, we will love with awareness and without the imprecision of a wonderful idea that does not reflect reality. I love horses for what they are and not for what I would have liked them to be. I would like them to do the same with me.

Would I like to improve my control, being able to err but without causing confusion, trying to understand myself a bit before trying to understand the horse? Good. If we want this, we have to be ready to do a few things that are apparently stupid.

We have a great power in our possession; imagination. To help it, we must put ourselves in real places but in imaginary situations. To imagine everything is unfortunately not efficient. The first condition is to put ourselves in a ring or wherever we usually work with our horse. The second, after that, is to imagine the horse and act as if he were really there.

In these conditions we can easily imagine a virtual interaction and test our physical responses. In order to be efficient, we must be convinced of our actions and be aware of our reactions, trying to understand where and how to intervene to improve our mental and physical responses. It requires a certain physical agility and a good mental dynamism. The most absolutely efficient way to do it is with two people who change roles between who interprets the horse and who the educator. In this way we will manage to see things and the difficulty from both points of view, correcting each other.

This system of training is innovative from the point of view of non-immediate interaction with the horse, and has the practical advantage of not causing stress to him due to the inexperience of his trainer. Clearly the scope of it is not to substitute the horse or to cover all the possible various reactions, but rather to make us aware of our limitations and expose our shortcomings before a direct encounter.

From the moment in which we start our interactions with the horse, one thing must be very clear: we are the leader, the one that has absolute control over him, or better, if this is our objective, the one who has the authority, the one he can trust and who is useful to follow his proposals. At this stage it is very important not to make mistakes or at least this is what we must make him believe. In this phase it is very important not to commit blunders, such as to ask for more than we can obtain, but always what we are sure of obtaining.

Let's imagine the case where in being with our horse at liberty, we have entered into the twenty-metre diameter ring for the first lesson and we want to stop our horse: to ask him this and to stay still on the spot without moving would be the greatest error that we could commit, as it would simply be impossible. He has greater strength than we do and a larger mass and it would be extremely arduous to hold him by force if he opposed us. But, above all, and take very careful note as this the most important thing, we would make him understand that he can 'not stop', that he can therefore not execute our requests, giving him this awareness. All this would put us in potential danger in that, whenever the horse wanted, or found himself in a position to capitalize on such an advantage, he will do so and, if he deems it necessary you can be sure he will do so.

For this reason, it is more difficult to re-educate than educate, because in re-education we face a horse who is dangerously aware of his own power, having subjugated humans many times and convinced that he can continue to do so (often, it can also be a horse who is insecure and suspicious and who eagerly awaits someone in whom they can trust)....

He is the leader and the more deeply rooted this conviction is in him; the more difficult it will be to gain his submission. If we are not credible, especially with stallions, we could find ourselves in dangerous situations.

Therefore never ask what we can't achieve and above all never lose sight of our objective, his collaboration, and to gain his trust.

Does this mean that we will never manage to stop our horse?

Of course not! We will manage to do a lot more, we will make him piaffe, passage, pirouette, do flying changes, jump or simply go on a wonderful hack, but all in due course and above all using a non-coercive method that predisposes and prepares the horse 'to do' both mentally and physically.

Firstly, if our objective was hypothetically 10, we can't get there by trying to explain to him '4+4+2=10, but rather 1+1+1+1+1+........ Then in future, when he has understood the value of 4 and its meaning obtained from 1+1+1+1=4, we can ask for more complex things. We should always be ready, whenever necessary to return to 1+1+1+1.....

Never lose sight of our objective: the horse's collaboration, and to gain its trust.

This means that we must set ourselves a goal that we can break down into elements. Look at a beautiful house and be aware of its structure, of the bricks, of the foundations and other features. We will acquire thus the awareness of the construction process. It won't be necessary to know the exact chemical composition of the cement but just its simpler properties that serve to hold the bricks together.

What then should we 'do'?

Simply, we should ask what we know we can achieve and convince him, that we have control of his actions.

We were saying that we can't ask him to stop, but we can ask him to go forward, even in a sudden manner, to make him canter, to make him change direction often and especially, not to let him take the initiative, like changing direction on his own, or stopping on his own. This we can do, and surely achieve and thus induce him to think that we have control over him, controlling his gaits and his direction, where control is never understood as an obligation.

The horse doesn't know that we will not ask him to stop because we are unable to stop him and so he doesn't even ask himself the question, but the question he will asks himself is 'but why can't I stop?' since if he did this of his own initiative we would be ready to make him go forwards again. In these terms things are very different. Do you understand how much that changes things? Radically.

But let's not rush ahead and firstly let's see how to start to interact.

We must not ask permission. Remember hierarchy? In asking for permission, we admit to being a lower level to him, therefore we go straight to the centre of the ring, without taking much notice of what he is doing. If he remains indifferent all we should do is observe and make sure that he doesn't come to us as we mustn't allow this yet. We require respect and we must be sure of having it. If he approaches us, we should send him away, cast him away without any hesitation. Especially if he is a stallion he must respect our space. To send him away isn't violent in his terms, if done right it is natural. This is enough to establish dominance. Just the fact that he has to move off rather than us and therefore yields to our pressure.

Our presence must have a weight, a tangible consistency, reflected in their attitudes, which must never be bold, in that they would not be tolerated because potentially dangerous.

Initially one can tolerate indifference, but not intrusiveness. Space is life. We are the leader.

We must establish the rules straight away; we can invade his space, but he can't ours, not yet, even he has to win trust. We must put ourselves on his level, but we must be master of the space. You don't know who I am and I don't know who you are, but perhaps we can collaborate, perhaps there could be something between us. Always leave this door open. Ours is not a definitive no but simply a 'let me understand who you are and I will explain who I am, but without excessive intimacy for the moment'.

See how things change, it is not up to us to gain his trust, in that it will automatically happen by expressing ourselves with their language, inspiring leadership and behaving ourselves in a coherent way.

We have to see things from a different point of view. It will be they who seek our trust, as long as we are and remain worthy of it, they will ask and we will concede; they will ask for rest and we will concede it gladly after they have executed our requests, they will ask for comfort (no pressure) and we will concede even this willingly as long as there is a correct response to our every tiny request (pressure), they will ask to enter into our circle, we will educate them in their own language but we will educate them to be disposed to our requests.

To do whatever is needed, not more and not less is the most complicated thing to carry out.

CHAPTER 12

Working at Liberty

What is it?

It is absolutely the most important stage of work with the horse. It is where we establish the rules and the rapport between him and us and where the relationship, which will be so important to our future together, must inevitably take place and be established.

When I first started this work and didn't know about ethology, I, like many people, had, a different approach to horses, which, with hindsight, I would now regard as reckless and dangerous. Today, even if a horse were brought to me for work straight from an international event, I would never start interacting with him before having done work at liberty. It is absolutely the best way for us to effectively get to know horses, and vice versa. The information that we get from work at liberty shows us, if we know how to look at it, the 'naked horse'; who he really is and how he relates to us. Please note that this is no small amount of information. Consider that a lifetime is sometimes not long enough to really know a person and that here, instead, we can get all this information on a horse within an hour. And increasing our knowledge of who we have in front of us will increase our safety – which should always be a priority.

(Beware of aggressive horses; we will deal with this subject in Chapter 16.)

Try to assimilate attitudes and movements that would be impossible to see directly once we are in the saddle.

Clearly, we will not be able to cover the whole sphere of possibilities with practical examples, but we will however, try to develop a flexible language that we can adapt from time to time to different circumstances.

We will start with work from the ground, which will be the easier for us to understand, since we will be able to maintain a physical distance that will allow us to observe and understand better, as opposed to work in the saddle, where the visuals are completely different. Let's therefore try to assimilate, through direct observation, those attitudes and movements that would be impossible to see directly once we are in the saddle, when we will have to associate what we have seen with what we will feel, transforming and associating sight with feeling, so as to always be aware of the 'how' of what the horse will do.

INITIAL OBJECTIVES

The first thing to understand is how the horse sees us – what attitude he assumes in relating to us and what role he means to take; whether he tends to be submissive, rebellious, and so on. We must always pay a lot of attention to his reactions and through these adapt our system of work, because the responses we receive will be our basis of departure for every possible new action. We should avoid making too many repetitive and confusing requests, and should also not to make too few requests, one far apart from the other, which would carry the risk of losing contact with him. We need to ask, trying to obtain a response as much in line as possible with our request, and allow him the correct interval of time so that he can absorb all this through his appreciation of the lack of pressure, the lack of further request and a comfortable state.

Let's immediately establish well-defined rules: respect is the starting point and is non-negotiable.

At the risk of being boring, I repeat again that we should not support the actions of the horse with repeated requests. In the uncertainty of whether the horse has understood us, and for the sake of good conscience, we can repeat our request once, but never more. After that, the request must be intensified in a growing and sudden manner until it simulates the aggression of the herd leader. When executing a request, the movement made must be minimal. Let's always bear in mind the sensitivity of the horse and that we are communicating in a way suited to him.

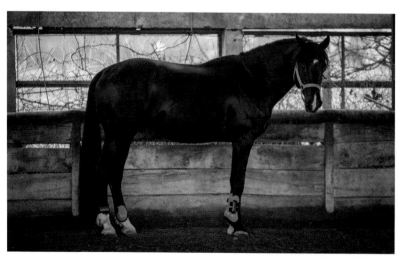

Maestoso waiting for a request.

We must seek to keep a neutral position (photo 1) and always maintain it whilst not requesting anything, and resume it once a request has been carried out. We must not allow the horse to stop and place himself in front of us. If this should happen, we should move sideways a little and with firm pressure if necessary (photos 3 to 5), compress space and re-send the horse forward, reassuming the neutral position.

Remember: communication in the herd; it suffices that a horse stops chewing for a moment to make the other understand that he is on thin ice and that it's time to change his intentions.

When we refer to moving our shoulders towards the horse's shoulders or haunches, this doesn't mean moving our whole body by walking but, keeping our legs in the same position, leaning slightly towards his shoulders or towards his haunches, in other words, leaning our shoulders a little to the right or the left.

Believe me, this is more than enough for the horse to feel us.

Do you remember 'lightness'? Little, smooth, light, minimal, gentle; these are the words which should spring to mind when we are asking something of the horse. 'Lightness' is what we should aim for in everything that we do, in that it is and always will be the most obvious choice for the horse. We must strive to do less and to make the horse do more.

In the same way, at the end of an exercise, we must not allow the horse to come towards us – not yet – he must first demonstrate that he is worthy of our trust.

We must have control in every situation; we must be absolutely convinced of it and, through repeated changes of direction, we will convince him as well.

In the beginning, don't ask him to stop in a certain point, not yet, remember: 'Never ask what you are not sure to obtain'.

WHAT EQUIPMENT DO WE NEED?

Usually I don't use anything – my body alone, in the correct attitude is sufficient – but initially I would strongly advise you to use a lunge line, which you could hurl about at the horse,

Sudden compression of the wall of air and flight.

holding one end in your hand, or a schooling whip, with which you could strike the ground at various distances from him to increase the pressure of the request.

It will absolutely not be necessary to touch the horse, or to ever hit him, to make him execute the requests. It is not needed; it is counterproductive, non-educational and can produce defensive reactions. The motivated intention of your actions will be more than enough to produce flight reactions.

The compression of a virtual air-wall between us and our horse; this is all we will need.

Let's remember that it is not what we do, but how we do it, that will make the difference. To always maintain an appropriate attitude is the most important thing. When aggression is necessary, a non-convincing attitude like 'Come on, come on then, move … what … why aren't you moving?' can have a contrary effect, whereas a motivated and convincing one like 'I AM GOING TO EAT YOOOOOOOOU!!!' will make even the boldest horse run like hell.

To hit a horse, whatever the motive, only serves the purpose of venting our frustrations and if this satisfies us in some way, then we need some sessions with a psychologist, or to play a hard rugby match before going riding: maybe this would put us back into a fit mental state.

A ring with secure fencing is always preferable to a rectangle for work at liberty. The absence of corners better reproduces the continuity of flight and, since there are no places in which the horse can wedge himself, efficiently establishes the concept of its futility.

THE PROCESS

We can make the horse learn numerous exercises with work from the ground, and we will look at these in more detail, but to give examples, we can teach him to move his haunches, move his shoulders, to go back, to flex his neck laterally and vertically, to change direction inwards or outwards, shoulder-in, and so on. We can teach all this from the ground (or almost) and we can do it with light requests, obtaining efficient responses. We can, but I personally tend to divide this into two clearly distinct phases.

In the first phase, I try to make the horse learn the essential things, that is to say those that I will need to start working safely in the saddle. These include, of course, to stop, to set off again quietly, the transitions to all three gaits, to change direction to the inside, flexion of the neck, and also to back-up (only in that it is indispensable to establishing submission, otherwise I'd willingly do without it). In this phase I would also include the whole series of necessary sensitizations and desensitizations.

I never teach the movements of the haunches or of the shoulder, or lateral movements like shoulder-in in that I am firmly convinced that these could be dangerous when initially starting the horse under the saddle.

When we mount the horse for the first time, the poor creature has already got a load to do to re-programme his own balance. Even if we didn't want him to do so he could, in defence or through incomprehension, execute these movements and, since he is not yet able to adapt his body to the weight of the rider, and based on the principle that the horse will not do what he is unaware of and doesn't know how to do, I far and away prefer to teach certain exercises later, or directly from the saddle.

The important point to understand is that the muscles and the balance that a horse uses to carry out certain exercises, with or without a rider, change radically, and before teaching him such exercises it will be necessary to prepare his musculature and, depending on his physical conformation, carry them out by making him assume the appropriate physical position for every specific exercise. These positions can easily be unnatural or non-instinctive to the horse.

We can obviously understand that, with a rider aboard, the horse will have to use his back and haunches differently so that this is not damaging to him, but we can be equally certain that, if it were left up to him to freely manage his own balance and assume positions more harmonious to him, he would not do so. He wouldn't do it because the horse is not born with a saddle and a rider and he would continue to assume all the attitudes which, for him, are simpler in that they are natural and less costly on an energetic level.

I often see children going to school with really heavy backpacks on their shoulders and not all of them curve their back to carry the weight – indeed, many do the opposite, arching it in the opposite direction. Now, to a child you can explain that this is a mistake, to a horse you can't. However we can, always through the use of language, ensure that it does not happen, by asking him to assume positions more consistent with that particular exercise. Since doing all this takes time and obviously it is impossible to teach it to the horse the first time we get in the saddle, I prefer to postpone these exercises until I am able to even partially manage the balance of the horse – that is, manage his balance through position obtained through communication. I absolutely never employ coercive instruments like draw reins but only proceed through the development of communication from the saddle and the use of a simple headcollar and a snaffle bit. But we will speak of this further later on. For the moment, let's be content with developing and understanding the language of work from the ground.

'First the position, and then the action.'

LICART

When we work with the horse, the best thing that we can do for him is to try to determine which is the best position and attitude in order to execute that exercise at that certain moment or phase of work, depending on his physical build and emotive tendencies. In this, I believe that we can be more or less in agreement. Of course, all these assessments must be made logically and with a fairly deep knowledge of the equine musculo-skeletal apparatus. This, however, if generalized, will not bear fruit. Only a specific analysis of the subject and therefore of his specific needs will lead us to adapt the 'positions' on a case-by-case basis, always using the procedures of stretching and de-contraction.

To make this concept clearer, for the same exercise but with differently built horses, you may tend to arrive at different 'positions' to achieve the same objective. By 'tend to' I mean that the 'positions' will never be fixed in time, but should indeed be adapted in line with changes in conditions and needs. The wisdom lies in being able to recognize which position we must make that specific horse assume for that specific exercise.

Further on in the book there are chapters that deal in greater depth with this difficult subject. For the moment, grasping the concept is sufficient.

Having understood all this – and it really is a lot – one can assess the 'how' to request or invite the horse to assume these positions, without considering for even one second coercive methods. At this point another world opens to us ….

THE POSITIONS OF OUR BODY FOR WORK AT LIBERTY

Our body speaks and can say many things.

We must first understand and manage to assume two basic attitudes, and change our state from neutral to active with reference to the space of air between us and our horse, compressing or expanding it. This space of air must always be considered absolutely tangible and never ethereal (the definition of air in the dictionary is: 'mixture of gases, especially nitrogen and oxygen which envelops the earth constituting its atmosphere'). Let's not fall into a common error of confusing a neutral attitude with a passive one; we must never be passive but rather relaxed in the confirming and not requesting phases. Passiveness is never useful for interaction.

- **Neutral attitude and neutral position (contact).** This is the attitude in which our mind is, in fact, serene and content with the horse's positive response. Such mental attitude must absolutely be translated into and correspond to a tangible bodily position to which the horse can refer; regular breathing, shoulders relaxed, absence of facial contractions, especially after intense phases or after aggression. Our change of state must be tangible. The space of air must not be compressed. Remember that the horse is observing us and, just as we base our actions on his reactions, the contrary will always true.
- **Active attitude and active position. In this case, we are asking something.** Our state changes from neutral to active and through our body we are compressing or expanding the space of air between us and the horse.

Neutral position.

Active position.

CHAPTER 13

Channelling Energy

Simple division.

To better understand where and how we direct our pressure during work at liberty, it is necessary for our purpose to divide the horse into three main parts. Of course this will be a simplified division; further on we will have the opportunity to carry out a more detailed analysis in order to achieve more refined objectives. For the moment what interests us is to divide the horse into:

· Head, neck and shoulders
· Trunk
· Hindquarters

and to try to see these parts as self-contained.

In this way it will become fairly instinctive for us to understand where to direct our pressures.

We will add a component to pressures in addition to:

· Space
· Intensity
· Time

Now we will also look at direction, which we will understand more intuitively.

If we consider the first three elements of space, intensity and time, as the grammar of implementation, then direction channels its effects.

Every time that we carry out an action we produce an energy that will be induced in the horse, which in turn will set off another. Now the resulting energy must be directed, because it will not always be channelled in the right direction. The direction of the request has the purpose of channelling the resulting energy of the correct response.

The point to understand is that the first essential thing we need is to manage to unleash energy, resulting from a request (in other words, the reaction). Without this it will not be possible to have any interaction because of the lack of action.

It is easier than it seems. If, for example, when working in the saddle we were to ask the horse to move his haunches to the inside and therefore as we proceeded with our request applying pressure with the outside leg, the horse were to react by going forward without moving his haunches, this should nonetheless be considered positive. In fact we have obtained a reaction, in that our request has set off a resulting energy. Now we must direct and channel this energy without extinguishing it.

Reaction is a valuable asset and must be treated as such. To attempt to block this flow with intent to extinguish it because it is not in line with our request would be damaging. and would threaten the will of the horse to react and to 'do'.

The flow needs to be channelled, for example by closing our hands just a little so as to limit rather than block the direction until it becomes uncomfortable, and at this point the flow will take another more open and comfortable route. This is not to say that the horse will take the direction we would like, but will try to drift towards the outside shoulder. No problem – maintaining these conditions we shall limit and render even that passage uncomfortable with our outside rein and so on until we channel him in the right direction. At that point we cease pressure by the decreasing of the aids to confirm and thereby create an association. I assure you that it is much more complex to say it than to do it.

The important thing is not to block the flow.

- Don't block the flow, but make it gradually uncomfortable.
- Channel it and lead it in a fluid way towards the desired direction.
- Say 'thank you' and always praise so that you can stimulate and increase the positive reaction, creating the correct reactive association, through the correct use of the descent of the aids.
- To obstruct, repress or abruptly block the reactive flow is never a good thing.
- Teach always with the aim of increasing the action and never promote its repression.

With work at liberty the concept is the same: of course it is obvious that the conditions and techniques change and now we will see how.

Let's take note and visualize where we are going to direct our pressure, already having very clear in our mind the exercise the horse must carry out.

I state that there are two strands of thought; the first is that, even after having made the request and having received a positive response, one should nonetheless maintain a position in line with the request (for example we move our shoulders laterally and towards the horse's haunches to make him go forward; once we have obtained a response we still remain moved towards his haunches to confirm the request) therefore we will have the position of our body still turned towards the haunches, maintaining a contact (never continuous pressure).

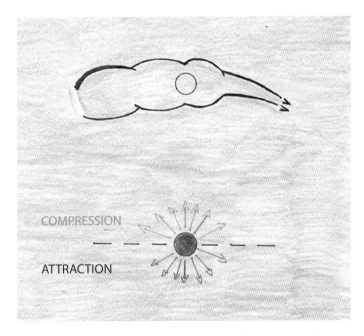

Possible actions of pressure or attraction.

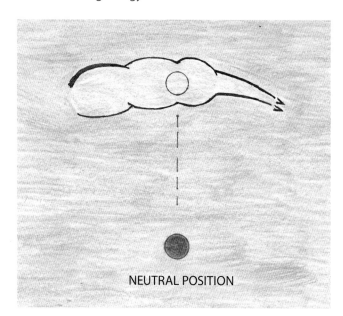

Neutral position.

NEUTRAL POSITION

The second line of thought is instead to return to a more neutral position and therefore more centred in line with the horse's back, neither turned towards the shoulders nor towards the haunches, always maintaining contact.

Personally, I have tried both of these with different subjects and both are effective and in line with the grammar of the language. In the first case we need to be careful not to fall into the temptation of offering too much support in the request and in the second case it is necessary to identify a neutral position that is effective. However, I prefer the second case.

I repeat that both work if used correctly, only, in my opinion, in the second example the fact that the horse should move on his own is reiterated with greater emphasis. To understand a 'neutral' or contact position is not easy. To explain it is even less so, in that the concept of contact is complicated. If it is too strong it becomes an involuntarily repeated request, and if it is too weak or absent … it is a bit like when the telephone line drops. We need to learn by making mistakes, relying on reaction which, in this case, is the simple awareness of being connected.

Sometimes a request is needed to establish the contact, as for example, to compress the space towards the horse; other times it is not – a gentle click of the tongue or a light slap of our hand on our thigh may suffice to get his attention.

So, head and shoulders, trunk, hindquarters, let's resume. In work at liberty our neutral position should be approximately just behind the withers. If we move laterally towards the quarters (direction), our intent will be that of making the horse move forwards. If we do it laterally towards the shoulders, we will communicate our intention for him to slow down, to stop, to change direction. If we compress the space in a given request, we will intensify the same, whilst if we move away we will produce a 'suction' effect, attracting him towards us. If we move away too far, breaking the contact, we will have to start again, and if the reactions of the horse are too strong, we must learn to dose down the pressure. Space, time, intensity and direction are all linked to one another and form the grammar of the language between the horse and us, to which we shall subject our body based on the reaction of the horse.

CHAPTER 14

Working Together: Going Beyond Requesting or Asking

For some time, it has been widely thought that we shouldn't request, whilst speaking the language of ethology, but inquire. The thinking behind this that to request is too absolute whilst to inquire is more correct, kinder and is expressed better in the language of the horse. Rubbish! Baseless nonsense.

Let's take two horses who don't know each other and put them together. Never, when I have done this, have I noticed kind inquiries, especially in the act of dominating. Here we have two options: either we try to understand horses and find the most logical way, trying to apply the grammar of the language, or – and this is fair – we scrape the bottom of the barrel of our ambiguity, trying to sublimate reality with a more idealized view (something that many of us are very good at doing).

The way in which horses express themselves is often hard, decisive and unambiguous, and this is their beauty. No false idealism, no ascetic charisma, but raw, pure and simple reality. Their mechanisms for survival and lightness of expressions are triggered and dictated by need and the obvious requirement of conserving energy and physical integrity, and cannot be misconstrued as sentimental kindness. Of course, we wouldn't dare to assess the outright battle between stallions to gain the right to transmit their genes:

'Ah, excuse me, pal, is this your harem? You know that I'm new around here and I'm just inquiring in case you would kindly let me mate with one of the girls.'

'Well of course, please go right ahead, there should be one in season over there.'

Strange then that one of them could die from his injuries sustained during this little chat between friends. Observe a herd and you will see what can happen when two mares contend for the dominant role; it isn't very subtle. Often, when a new subject introduces himself into the herd, many months can pass before he begins to be accepted and this has nothing to do with dominance or respect or another's living space. It is much more complicated and he could be bound to the role of the outcast for a very long time, even up to the extinction of several dominant generations. The herd is an army, not a recovery class.

The grammar of the horse's language has very little to do with philosophy. The concept of democracy has a philosophical root and it is a purely human discipline, derived from the fact that our minds are able to process an impressive quantity of impressive concepts. Moreover, during evolution we have developed concepts that often go against the rules of Mother Nature. Compassion, charity and love are all concepts outside of the evolutionary process. The concept that I would like to express is that nature works in a drastic ways, and has always done so. In nature, if a subject is weak or in difficulty he is not cured, but eliminated in order that his genes are not transmitted. We are going against the system of natural selection in curing

In nature, if a subject is weak or in difficulty, he is not cured, but eliminated in order that his genes are not transmitted.

the sick, helping those in need when they wouldn't manage by themselves and especially in being able to elaborate and conceive thoughts as immense as equality and charity. All of this is unnatural – yes, it's wonderful, but not natural – just as it is not natural for the horse to live and collaborate with humans. The introduction of the horse into life with humans, the taming, the training, are all actions for which humans must assume total responsibility. In so-called 'natural taming', there is nothing natural. There has to be the know-how of an educated, ethical and intelligent human.

Let's not, then, scramble up tortuous philosophical paths, but follow them just far enough to render us a little more aware.

GO AWAY

'Go on, go over there, shoo!'…..Even if the more correct expression – the one that best conveys the idea – is: 'Move yourself wherever you want, but further away from me, give me some space', please'. This is an attitude that we must have when we enter the ring, positioning ourselves in the centre, should the horse, of his own initiative, approach us. Only a few moments are needed to establish a rapport of dominance and this happens in the same way as when we put two horses in the same paddock for the first time.

Let's always remember that the first request, the one to move a little, should be carried out with 'lightness', and should absolutely not, in fact, be seen as an absolute request but as an inquiry, a polite conversation, and all is well if the horse responds in a positive manner. But it can happen that the horse tries to react to our request with an attempt at aggression and it

When the horse shows a defiant attitude we need an energetic act of aggression. In this case I threw a lunge rein at him.

is important to read the signs. If his reaction is that of moving his ears back, trying to intimidate us because he doesn't like what we have just asked, we must be ready to respond 'tit for tat'.

This is where it is decided whether we will dominate or be dominated. We must be absolutely convinced of what we are doing because if we can't convince ourselves, imagine the horse. In this case, if we can't manage to pose as head of the herd, we should pull out our convinced predator instinct and use it to send the horse away, throw the lunge line at him or hit the ground with the schooling whip in a decisive manner, roar, whilst leaping towards him like a feline, in short do something that induces the horse to fear us. We will then have time, proceeding with the work, to regain his trust, re-donning the robes of a wise head of the herd. This step is fundamental and he must yield space, and this is not negotiable.

Note, I repeat again, if you are dealing with an exceptionally aggressive horse, do not start any action without having read that part of Chapter 16 that deals with this subject.

But the opposite could easily happen – that is, the moment we enter the ring, the horse could take himself to the furthest point from us, giving evident signs of restlessness, or even try to run off, going into a mad canter around us. In this case, we divide our work into three phases.

- **First phase:** Remain still, with a relaxed attitude, and let him do it. This is usually enough in that, after a while, he realizes that no real danger exists and that, in any case, running away is useless and therefore starts to calm down and accept our presence.
- **Second phase:** After having waited a reasonable time, without the horse having given any signs of calming himself down, try to make him change direction repeatedly. This type of exercise should break the action derived from his survival instinct that makes him flee uncontrollably and, in a short while, he will regain a more alert and serene attitude.
- **Third phase:** If the horse, while passing the phases described above, still does not give signs of calming himself down (very rare), we will need to carefully assess his physical state and decide whether we should exit and try again another time, in that a horse is capable of running until he makes his heart burst, and we don't want to kill him, just educate him. Don't worry about having to interrupt 'unfinished' work – clearly this action should not be the rule, but we always need to assess the pros and cons. If his psycho-physical well-being is at risk, it is best to interrupt. We will always have time to recuperate. Let's remember that the horse has a strong spirit of adaptation and, once he has understood that no danger exists, he will be happy to change his behaviour. This will also be useful to us, maybe revising some phases of work. Therefore, be ready to change.

Once the horse has started to calm himself down, it is important that there is no type of interaction on our part; let's leave him quietly to stop and take a long break, the length of which will depend on the degree of the horse's stress . He is accepting our presence with a change of state, which is what we wanted, and the pause will reinforce this. (If the horse is really tired, our first lesson can safely end here; we can leave the work area and start again after a few hours, or the next day. Once, it took me three days until a horse accepted me and I had to cling firmly to the theoretical concepts, without wavering, after which the work resumed a 'normal' course.)

At this point the horse will have yielded space or accepted our presence and will find himself at a distant point from us and we can proceed.

Let's ask him to go forwards, changing our position from neutral to moving towards his quarters (moving our shoulders laterally to the right or left, towards his quarters without compressing the space between us and the horse). If he advances, let's say from walk to trot, we return to the neutral position; if he doesn't advance we repeat the request with the same intensity. If this is not sufficient, which can easily happen, we move ourselves in an abrupt and sudden manner towards the horse, always in the direction of his quarters, this time compressing the space that separates us in a sharp way (intensity), always being very careful not to put ourselves in a position of danger. Our movements have to be more decisive the less reactive the horse is and vice versa; a decisive request should be more than sufficient to produce impulse, indeed the horse should be inclined to escape as if there were a tiger in hot pursuit. Always remember that we should never follow him, as eating him is not our goal. Once we have received the desired reaction we should return as soon as possible to our neutral position. Of course, we should not remain immobile. The horse moves and we should try to follow him by making in turn our own circle of a few metres, seeking to maintain our neutral position. Dynamism is needed. Once we have managed to obtain a regular gait for a few consecutive circuits without him trying to escape or slow down and change direction, we can consider ourselves satisfied – we have achieved a communicative skill, indeed two; there was the primary one, the yielding of space and now we have started to manage space through the movements of the horse.

If he escapes, let him by all means run off, while we stay in our neutral position and, after a while, once he has regained a more tranquil gait, for example a good working trot, we make him change direction.

However, before starting the change of direction, we need to study the mechanics of the horse a little.

Let's better understand how he works.

Brusque changes of direction.

CHAPTER 15

Natural Flexions

All horses are asymmetrical, like us.

This is not a trivial matter, but we often tend not to give a lot of importance to it, which is a mistake that may lead us to draw the wrong conclusions, mistaking the difficulty the horse has in executing a movement for a lack of will or problems deriving from an altered mental state. I often hear ineptitude blamed, because a horse managed an exercise well on one rein, whilst on the other, he didn't want to know. This is not ineptitude it's natural asymmetry – they are made like that!

Let's take the example of a horse with natural flexion to the right and see what we can expect of him.

A horse with right flexion will have the following prevalent characteristics:

- Head turned towards the right.
- Left shoulder inclined to escape towards the outside.
- Haunches that travel towards the right and, as a consequence, the right hind leg engages more than it pushes and the left hind leg pushes more than it engages.
- On the left diagonal, he is inclined to advance more.

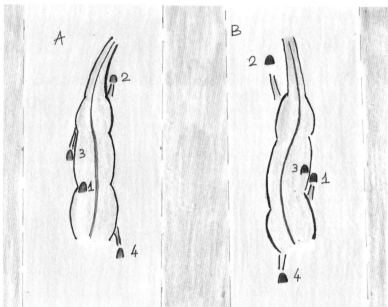

Example of the two diagonals of trot in a horse with right flexion. Note how the spinal cord resembles two 'S's, of which one is upside down, with various degrees of curvature. Hence:
A1: modest engagement
B1: deep engagement
A4: lesser thrust
B4: bigger thrust
A2: limited extension
B2: ample extension

The sensation that all of us have experienced, even without executing complex exercises, but simply riding on the right rein or the left rein, is that of having a different horse every time we change rein, and it's a correct sensation.

All the situations that I have described above will tend to be accentuated with the increasing difficulty of the exercise – the more complex the exercise that is requested of the horse, the more he will tend to assume the more comfortable position for himself.

For example (assuming that we are right-handed), if we had to do something simple with our left hand, like grabbing a still object such as a tennis ball, we wouldn't have much of a problem, but if the ball were moving, in order to catch it in the air, surely we would instinctively use our right hand. The horse does the same thing every time he feels himself in trouble, and understanding this puts us in a position of being able to help him to develop his rectitude (straightness) by the use of constructive and focused gymnastics.

This type of gymnastics, which is initially de-contractive, can only be partially applied during work from the ground, where the movements of human and horse are separate, and will find its natural application during work under saddle, when we can seek to make the horse assume certain corrective positions in loosening-up movements. Gymnastics without movement could be quite helpful for helping the horse to acquire the initial process of training, and would therefore be partially useful if viewed as education to basic reactions, but nothing more.

The symbols ')))' indicate the intensity of the action executed by the horse. For example in a right flexed horse engagement of the rear right will be larger than that of the rear left, etc.

One can argue that if 'the study of language is the essence of interaction, movement is its application'.

Immobility in equitation spells disaster. I was forgetting something important: of course to achieve this, as a rule, a lifetime isn't enough. It's a bit like us not 'being' ambidextrous but trying to become it (if one is born like it, it does not count).

Having said that, it is necessary to take note of real de-contraction, which must precede every exercise where impulsion will support execution, and will allow us a glimpse of rectitude through the harmonious flexibility of the actions. But this is not yet the moment to delve too far into this subject; suffice to say that a horse who is bent to the right will have certain attitudes and, consequently, we will notice a penchant towards certain reactions.

On the right rein (horse bent to right) – reactions to pressure towards the front end.
The shoulder will tend to take itself towards the outside, the head towards the inside, along with the haunches. In work at liberty he will instinctively execute a change of direction towards the outside in counter-flexion and will show a higher sensitivity to pressure towards the shoulders, yielding and responding in an excessive manner, taking them away from the point of

request. We will have both the sensation of having his attention (head to the inside) as well as the sensation that, nevertheless, the horse tends to move away from us; that he escapes along the track furthest away. On the request to halt, he tends to stop himself obliquely, showing us his haunches, with the shoulder furthest away, and the head turned towards us.

On the left rein – reactions to pressure towards the front end. The head tends to be turned towards the outside, with the base of the neck pushing the shoulders towards the inside, haunches turned to the outside. In work at liberty the horse will easily execute changes of direction towards the inside because of loss of balance. We will have the sensation that he tends to avoid our gaze (carrying his head to the outside); our pressures towards the shoulder are initially well understood and the shoulders do not tend to escape, indeed, it will seem as if the horse is leaning towards our request, providing a tangible contact, as in the request for a halt. But if the pressure is increased, we will have the feeling of rejection and opposition, with changes of direction to the inside. On the request for halt, he tends to direct the haunches towards the outside, falling on the inside shoulder, obliquely towards us.

On the right rein – reaction to pressure towards the rear end. The right hind leg instinctively tends to take itself under the

ABOVE: Preamble: the horse tends to channel its energy according to where it usually flows with greater frequency and intensity: this means that by applying pressure in different points it will, through mere convenience, follow the tendential flow. This reaction is often badly interpreted or misunderstood by the rider who looks for absurd explanations for non-cooperation and lack of willingness on the part of the horse, punishing it when instead a re-education in the balancing of the flows is the solution. To punish a reaction in his willingness to act is the worst thing we can do. Natural reaction to pressure on the right shoulder: in this case the horse's reaction is more or less in line with the pressure.

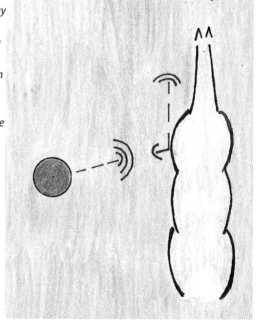

RIGHT: Natural reaction to pressure on the left shoulder: the pressure tends to be partially rejected and transferred to forward movement.

mass, pushing in a restricted way, whilst the left hind moves away from it, increasing the push; the haunches are curved stably towards the inside. On requesting him to go forwards he will advance more on the left diagonal, with the haunches directed towards us. The haunches tend to reject pressure the more that pressure tries to move them to the outside (rotation of the haunches around the shoulders) giving vent to a forwards movement towards the left diagonal (every reaction takes the route where it can run more smoothly, *see* Chapter 13, Channelling Energy).

On the left rein – reaction to pressure towards the rear end. The left hind leg pushes more than it engages and struggles to take itself under the mass, whilst the right engages more than it pushes and receives the thrust of the left without too much opposition to it. On requesting him to go forwards he will react by moving his haunches away from the pressure, tending to step across under himself to perform a rotation of the haunches on the shoulder.

This means that it is 'normal' that, in applying the same kind of pressure, we should receive opposite reactions to it, simply by changing rein.

Of course, head-neck, shoulder and haunches are also connected and their interactions accentuate attitudes.

It will be quite simple, in a horse who is bent to the right, to make him execute a rotation on the haunches on the left rein, even if the inside shoulder tends to fall in, and very difficult to do on the right rein, where he will naturally bring his shoulder forwards towards the outside.

We must add something else which is very important. Let's try to really understand this part.

Natural reaction to pressure on the right haunches: the pressure tends to be partially rejected and redirected forward to the left shoulder.

Natural reaction to the pressure towards the left haunches: the pressure is well-channelled but since the left shoulder has a tendentially greater lateral movement compared to the haunches and therefore a wider channel for the flow (considering that the flow tends to go forwards) part of the energy will be redirected towards it.

In work under saddle, this asymmetry of the horse can cause us to have a false bilateral contact in that, on a right-flexed horse, we will tend to have a greater contact on the left and almost nothing on the right. This, over time, will cause us many headaches. As a consequence we will tend to 'straighten out' the neck without gymnastics, applying therefore our visual sense of rectitude. Doing so, over time, our sensitivity will become distorted, and also using the left (outside) rein will become complicated. Because every time we try to get an outside contact, we receive a small outside flexion which, in turn, will cause us to leave the outside contact in favour of the inner one, so as to get the feeling that the horse is more 'straight'. These are the simple laws of physics, nothing more.

Let's imagine a long stick that is a bit twisted towards the right, with two cords tied to one end. In order to make it appear straight, we must exert a force from its convex side (left) and none from its concave side (right). Now, if it is done for just a short time, this exercise will have no effect, but done over a long period it will result in an induced and enhanced asymmetry. The really important thing here is that we are not doing this with an inanimate object, but with a receptive muscular structure that will initially tend to straighten itself out, and we will subsequently have an intensification of the muscular mass in opposition, resulting in a gradual desensitization, not only of the horse but also of the rider. Over time, trying to have a straight horse, without the appropriate gymnastics, does nothing but create and increase an unbalanced and unlearned support. The rider, as well as the horse, will be inclined to desensitize the left contact, fortifying an opposite and contrary musculature in the horse (contracting the right side of the neck) and a direct one for the rider (contracting the left arm musculature, flexing the spine towards the right and overusing the left contact).

This means that, as well as learning the language and all it entails, and also learning to assume the correct attitudes, in order to avoid misinterpretations of reactions, we also need to

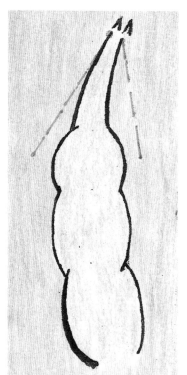
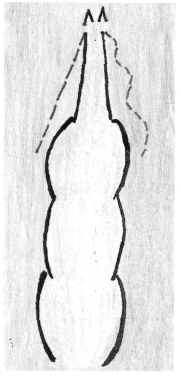

In a right flexed horse our instinctive reaction will be to increase contact on the left rein in an effort to make the horse go visually 'straight'. This will in time create an induced support to the left with loss of contact on the right rein, which will reinforce the musculature in opposition.

learn the 'biomechanics' of the horse so as to recognize his responses of convenience, related to his asymmetry.

A study of the language cannot exist as an end in itself, if it does not take into account the reactive learning linked to the behavioural asymmetry derived from the natural mechanics of the horse.

Now we can close the circle; we have all the elements we need to be able to make a correct interpretation of the horse's reactions.

Let's always start from the concept that we manage the space inside which the horse moves and, through this space, the movements of the horse himself; never the other way around.

CHANGE OF DIRECTION TOWARDS THE OUTSIDE

Now let's move ourselves slightly towards and against the shoulder or the head of the horse and, if we don't receive the desired reaction, let's ask again by taking ourselves out of the neutral position to the position towards and against the shoulder or head of the horse. If the horse changes direction then all is well and we should put ourselves as soon as possible back to our neutral position, passing the horse's haunches whilst he changes direction, leaving him space to move off. If this doesn't happen, we must decidedly and quickly reduce the space between us and the horse (increase intensity – against – towards – sudden decrease of space and compression of the wall of air), cutting the ring in the direction of his nose, so as to compress the air interposed between us. Having done that, we should return to a neutral position past the haunches of the horse. If the horse, on the compression of space and therefore the increase of pressure, just goes past us, no problem – let's not press him too hard, let's take up our neutral position and try again, this time cutting him off further ahead, towards his nose. We should have the sensation that during the request the air is compressed to the point of becoming a 'wall', in front of which the horse cannot have any other reaction than to turn back.

Once we have a change in direction, having resumed our position, we observe the horse and bring him back to a calm but determined gait; it can be walk, trot or canter depending on the circumstances, but initially trot is the more advisable gait since it is the easiest to keep active and can be sustained for a long time whilst also respecting the warm-up phase of the horse. Our management of space is expanding.

Our objective is that of making the horse re-establish his gait without supporting him. The procedure is always the same. After the change of direction, let's say that the horse has gone into walk, so let's ask him to take the trot again by placing our shoulder slightly towards his haunches. If he goes into trot we return to our neutral position. If he escapes, we also return to our neutral position; we should not try to stop him by placing ourselves towards his shoulder – we could do it but if he doesn't react in a correct manner we would have to insist right up to making him change direction and then would have to start all over again. Therefore, we should try to stay in our neutral position and, after a short while the horse should stop escaping and return to a working trot. If this doesn't happen we can try to use repeated and frequent changes of direction, which should result in making the horse continuously change his perspective without fixing himself on one idea: 'escape'. If instead, his reaction isn't decisive enough, we mustn't make the mistake of asking more than twice, but quickly carry out a decisive action of compression of space, followed by a return to our neutral position.

We shouldn't ask too much, or too many things. We don't create confusion and, before asking something, we make sure that he is in a good receptive state, that is, we have his atten-

Change of direction towards the outside.

tion and he is fairly calm. If we don't have these conditions, we should try to find out why. If he runs off without apparent reason, let him do so until he understands for himself that this action is futile. The reasons for this have been dealt with previously.

MAINTAINING THE GAIT

The principle is always the same: don't support him to make him do it, but indicate, ask, check, without being involved in doing it; it's the horses job, not ours. Accepting the fact that our efforts cannot be part of the practical execution, we must make sure it does not happen, but as they say: 'twixt cup and lip …'.

As we have seen, to educate the horse to give the correct reactions means more importantly to educate ourselves, and often the instinct to participate and therefore create support is very strong. Impulse cannot be created; it is already present in the horse and the more our actions are repeated in a continuous way, the more the horse will get used them (process of desensitization).

Important rule: when we ask something, we must be sure that this is within the horse's capabilities and, having established that this is so, we visually imagine the correct reaction of the horse and seek it from him without compromise. For example, if we request a transition from walk to trot, this must be as sharp and balanced as possible. That is to say that he shouldn't just fall into a trot and neither should he run off into canter. If his transitions are listless, we should make our requests grow exponentially until they simulate aggression, whilst if he escapes into canter we invert our pressure, bringing it towards his shoulder until he adopts the correct reaction, after which we should return to our neutral position.

We will look now at what to do if the horse tends not to maintain his gait, showing 'laziness'. Our instinct would be to repeat our request, placing ourselves more towards the haunches and moving closer to him, perhaps culminating, in our attempt to help him, at running closely after him to make him go forward or until he maintains a semblance of trot. Hey presto! We have discovered how the horse can make us the ones to trot!! This means that the horse isn't aware (since it has not yet been expressed) of our potential – our capacity to be, of course, fair and understanding, but equally to be intentionally aggressive and dominant. We must always offer him the choice of collaboration and always keep this door wide open. Failing this, the chance that lightning may strike 'out of the blue' should be included as a possible response in our attitudes, the meaningful and conscious use of which will be up to us.

Therefore, we ask once, we repeat the request in case there has been a misunderstanding as a consequence of distraction and then, if the horse continues to not maintain his gait and as a consequence falls 'asleep' on the request, this is the moment to carry out an aggressive action towards his haunches, which shall be all the more decisive, the less reactive he is.

If our action has been correct, the horse's natural response will be to run like hell. Also here, let's not commit the mistake of prolonging our action, which should indeed be interrupted immediately. Leave him for a moment to let off pent-up steam, and remain quiet and calm in the centre of the ring then, as soon as conditions permit, ask him to return to walk. If he is still tense, wait until he calms down, after which ask carefully (in that his parameters of attention may now be very sensitive), to take himself again into trot, positioning our shoulders towards his haunches. The horse will certainly be inclined to increase his gait or at least to maintain it. If this is not the case, we repeat the aggression, but without abusing it. It is not necessary to repeat this more than two, or a maximum of three times, as this would mean that there exists a different problem that we haven't yet understood.

Aggression, or better put, the sudden compression of the space between us and the horse, is like the lesson to the leg under saddle and produces the same result, to rebalance the aids, restoring the concept of lightness.

In fact, the lesson to the leg should be carried out where, for various reasons, the horse shows heaviness and habituation to aids and requests. We should gently apply the whip on the rear, with sudden increases of intensity until we get a better response.

The lesson to the leg, like aggression, should be carried out very few times in the life of the horse and essentially serves to rebalance the dormant communication parameters. Consistency of requests, on the other hand, is usually applied in all cases where hyperactivity occurs and which require desensitization.

Our goal must never be to sensitize or desensitize a horse, but to bring *balance* to the aids and *harmony* to his reactions.

Structure of the Language to Maintain the Horse's Gait

Premise: I have often used the words 'language' and 'grammar', which are terms normally referring to the spoken word. Clearly my use of these terms refers to non-verbal communicative actions that also have a linguistic and grammatical structure. It is therefore wrong to interpret the act of communication solely through words, because our brain processes this information and the resulting actions in a manner not appropriate to body language. Body language must be understood, translated and expressed in a different manner with different mental processes. Willpower has no effect on changing these processes; what we must do is simply get used to using and interpreting body language again. So, when I speak of language and grammatical rules, I am never referring to those of the spoken word but always of non-verbal communication. The main characteristic of body language resides in immediacy, whilst verbal language doesn't often provide for it. As a consequence, it is very important to approach actions and reactions in a very simple and not over-reasoned way, and begin to manage them by the instinct that is inside us, even if it is somewhat dormant.

Initially, we will need to analyse all the input and output information. This will delay us in our interpretation and expression. However, body language is part of our background. Through use, it will increase, and as a consequence, so will our effectiveness in communicating.

Must we stop to reason? No, I don't want this! But, let's try to do it before and after. During the action, let's be driven by our instincts, using our body language. Obviously, it will have to be a re-educated language – the one we are equipped with (the body language of the primate) isn't always in line with the horse's one.

Now let's review the request's sequence.

- Request: our shoulders positioned towards the horse's haunches (to be repeated a maximum of twice: request – neutral position – request).
- Aggression or compression of space (starting after the second request).
- Neutral position or contact (wait until the horse calms down and request walk, positioning our shoulders in the direction of the horse's shoulders or head.
- Our shoulders towards the horse's haunches to bring him to trot.
- Neutral position (if the horse still doesn't maintain the gait, repeat the whole sequence, increasing the intensity of aggression).

This should be more than sufficient to produce a situation in which the horse has self-carriage. Not only this, but by using this system, we can regulate the gaits, gaining confidence in using pressure. A gentle request towards the head or towards the haunches can produce a decrease or increase in the gait, whilst a sharper request will determine a lower or higher transition.

The horse will, inasmuch as he can, respond to lightness, provided that we manage to keep him balanced in his reactions and therefore responsive to requests, but we must always be ready to compress the space suddenly at every hesitant reaction.

If we are consistent in our way of communicating, the horse will reward us with correctness, which will naturally bring him onto a path of trust, led by our consistency and driven by his innate instinct of belonging, thereby causing feelings of collaborative contentment.

It is in the horse's nature to feel that he is an active part of the herd, finding a dimension as an individual through collaboration or dominance.

PAUSES AND IMMOBILITY

Pauses are the confirmation that what has just happened is correct, and reinforces our neutral position. It is indispensable for a correct education and encourages 'execution'.

The pause is the cessation of all requests, which then returns the horse to an instinctively

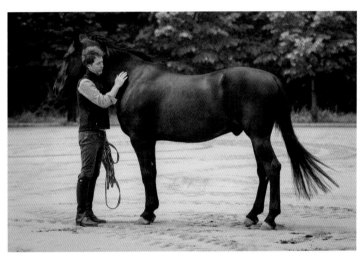

Pauses.

welcome condition that relies heavily on the first law 'to save energy', and if work carried out well always results in a pause, then it follows that willingness to 'execute' will follow in perfect harmony. A gentle stroke can reinforce the pause. We should avoid noisy pats on the neck which, although tolerated, are not normally liked. The pause is the confirmation and the king of all rewards.

Again, the pause should not be understood as a purposeful end to the exercise, but as an interruption of requests, and can also be manifest in such forms as going down to walk after an exercise, with loose reins and a stretched neck, or going down to a working trot after passage. A pause should be read as a noticeable reduction of the exercise's intensity. A rewarding pause can also happen within an existing exercise by a sensitive reduction of intensity. Important! For communication purposes, the horse should be rewarded because he undertook to do the exercise, even if he didn't do it in a correct or perfect way.

His willingness should be rewarded and his willingness will increase! Nothing is so beautiful and pleasant as having a collaborative horse, who follows our requests through rewarding communication. This is a solid base for good equitation.

Be careful though, not to confuse the pause with the halt, in that the latter is in an active phase and doesn't always precede a passive phase, for example: trot-halt-trot. Let's teach him to stop himself in a correct manner and reinforce the concept of immobility.

He is not to be allowed to stop himself whenever he likes; if he does so we should be ready to take him suddenly forward, especially with horses who are too desensitized.

How do we ask for halt? During the work we have performed until now, we have already done it. When? At every request for change of direction.

Effectively, it is not a real and true halt, but rather that moment of suspension where the horse can change direction. This, or even a second before, would be the time to take away our pressure.

Of course the horse could still change direction … no problem, but since this is not what we want, we should be ready to ask him to change again and again in shorter lapses of time, but with less intensity.

In doing this the horse loses momentum and his actions will become calmer and calmer in a way that makes it easier for us to calculate the 'moment' (remember when we spoke of timing) in which to take away our pressure and the horse will stop, taking himself out of a stalemate situation with which he is not comfortable. Having said that though, he should not be allowed to stop himself however and whenever he wants, turning his back to us or positioning himself in front of us (natural flexion). He should do it remaining on the circumference of the circle, positioned laterally to us, giving us his side. If these conditions are not met, we should send him forwards and ask again.

The halt doesn't mean 'stop at your leisure however and whenever you want', it means 'immobility'.

This request is very important and must be well understood by us before teaching it so it can be executed correctly. If the horse is trotting on a circle in the ring, the moment we ask for a halt (immobility), he should not stop himself and then turn – that is not what we have asked for – nor should he turn himself and then stop. Immobility must be precisely as requested; he can do it without difficulty and must not set off again on his own initiative.

Right from the start of ground work, stopping must be a finite concept and must not mean anything other than that. If a horse is insecure, he will tend to set off again or do something else. In this case we need to be careful about applying pressure involuntarily, and ensure that there is a mutual understanding of the neutral zone. In these cases it may be necessary to repeat change of direction a few times, gradually relaxing the pressure. When we do manage to achieve the desired result, we should interrupt all our actions for a long time, going imme-diately into the neutral position with a relaxed attitude. In other words, we must put the horse into a comfortable situation, and the more intense the work session has been, the more this pause will be appreciated. So the halt, for him, will become one of the most rewarding situ-ations because, in the prolonged halt, he will find himself in an effectively comfortable posi-tion, without effort, requests or the like. Thus the pause assumes the value of confirmation and reward.

After a significant pause, we should change our state and pass from the neutral position to that of placing ourselves towards the haunches to send him forward. The walk is, in this case, preferable but should he set off in trot, no problem – next time we will simply ask more gently, positioning ourselves a bit less and, as soon as we have reached a stable situation and contact, we should again ask for immobility. If instead he is not ready to set off again, as always, we should ask again, after which our actions should be increased suddenly as already explained. It's like saying 'Relax as much as you want, but pay attention to me'.

Clearly, this exercise is more or less simple depending on the type of horse. With some types, I call them the 'ecologists' (those who make the saving of energy their principal goal in life), it will be far too easy. We must be careful, with this type of horse, not to fall into his trap which, in our noble efforts to help him, will instinctively cause us to reinforce our request, thereby creating the basis of heaviness and desensitization. Sudden changes of our state, all the way up to convinced aggression, will be the cure for this type of horse, in the same way that many repetitions of requests will be the cure for an over-sensitive horse. If we think about it, the attitude that we should adopt is often the converse of the one prompted by our instinct.

Usually, horses start to collaborate straight away and find themselves perfectly at ease in this type of situation, in that it is an integral part of their way of relating and, the more horses have (or have had) a social life in a herd, the more these mechanisms are present in them. This work is much easier with such horses (we can obtain sharper responses in them) than with horses in whom forced isolation (whether confined to a box, or simply because the horse has grown up on his own) has provoked insecurity arising from the inability to interact because of the physical lack of confrontation.

We will never substitute the education of the herd. We are not horses and, even if we try, through ethological study, to behave like them, for them we never will be. Horses are perfectly capable of distinguishing one of their own from a human being and, only through our attitude will it one day be possible to make them accept us as beings on whom they can rely and to whom they can give their most precious gift, trust.

Immobility, pause: this concept must be clear, to us and them.
Let's introduce another concept.

Finite and Infinite

First law – a request will be followed by an action, which must persist as such and therefore last until the subsequent request of interruption, which will end said action (infinite action).
Second law – a request will have, as a consequence, an action which must persist as such until its completion (finite action).

These two laws allow a third one, the 'compound' request, which is a combination of two or more requests which can co-exist between themselves without losing their individual proper-ties. One can therefore have finite actions during an infinite action and vice versa.

Every request and therefore every action 'finite, infinite or compound' is broken down into 'instants' and every instant or 'moment' is the broken down snapshot of the action on which interaction is possible.

The request for trot is an infinite action, that is, the action must persist without being interrupted. The peculiarity of infinite actions is that they must continue without the need of repeated support of the request.

The requests for change of direction, like that of half-pass, shoulder-in and so on are finite actions that end on completion.

The characteristics of finite actions are that they follow the request (which should, however, be lightened or intensified according to the reply of the horse and never remain static) and that they are interrupted when the response is completed.

Immobility is therefore a request which foresees an infinite action and must always be treated as such.

All clear? Let's make an example of an infinite action.

When we ask for a halt, we do not maintain the request so that the horse stays still, just as when we ask for a transition to trot, we don't continue to ask so that the horse maintains it – he must support the action on his own. This 'infinite' action lasts until a new request for a transition.

CHANGE OF DIRECTION TOWARDS THE INSIDE

I have gone on a lot about how to compress space. Now, to be able to execute this exercise, we must learn another skill: 'drawing in'.

This exercise can be very hard in that, as well as learning the skill of drawing in; we need the horse to give us a pinch of trust.

The first action to carry out will be that of drawing back. If we have established a good contact, the horse should start to approach and bring himself towards us as if he had been 'sucked in'. At this point, while continuing to draw back, we take ourselves towards the horse's head until we can see his outside shoulder, at which point we should stop stepping back and apply a pressure to it.

The critical phase consists in letting the horse's head cross over the median line which connects our bodies so as to be able to apply pressure to the outside shoulder.

Having identified the critical moment, we should work on it to avoid creating misunderstanding. So let's look at the problem by slowing down the execution. It can help to execute this exercise in walk, especially on the more difficult rein (see Chapter 15, Natural Flexions). We should proceed calmly, bringing the horse close to his critical point. If he tends to slow down, turning himself towards us, we should continue to draw back, luring him to a more inside track, therefore placing ourselves towards his head, always drawing back a bit, placing ourselves laterally, until we arrive at his outside shoulder in a way that allows us to direct pressure to it, and after the reaction (change of direction) we should pass towards his haunches to confirm the movement, subsequently regaining the neutral position. At this point we need to keep repeating the exercise until it acquires fluidity.

The objective is always to understand the effective difficulties, which can be either ours or the horse's, and to help him overcome them. To do this we need to make a logical analysis of his reactions, to understand them and to act accordingly, always trying to place the horse in the best condition to execute the given exercise. This requires an overall picture, the so-called 'seeing at a glance', which, of course, one needs time to perfect. Meticulousness will need

Attraction.

to replace instinct, analysing the problem step-by-step, breaking it down into lots of snap-shots, going over it and seeking the correct execution, applying the right variables at the right moment, using 'slow-motion', so that, later on, instinct may come back and play its vital role. The 'positive' thing, if we want to call it that, consists in the fact that all the mistakes we make during our learning process can easily be remedied, provided of course that we know how to recognize them and correct them.

MOBILITY AND CONTROL OF THE HEAD

The horse's head is extremely mobile. On it, both eyes and ears also have great mobility and directionality but, if requested these can also be directed towards a point of interest by the movement of the head as a whole.

The lateral movement of the head measures about 300° from one side to the other; it has considerable range of vertical movement, and its substantial weight is supported by strong neck muscles.

A horse does not use his head as a battering ram and it is therefore not considered to be a defence weapon but, if by accident, in a sudden movement, it hit us, it could kill us. A right hook from Mike Tyson would be a caress in comparison. We should therefore give it due attention when working within its range of action.

Through a light pressure the horse learns to yield and to follow the hand. In this photo, one can see that he is executing the exercise but is not yet very convinced. His expression is not serene. We need to further gain his trust to render the exercise really effective.

Our aim will be that of mobilizing the head and drawing it towards us.

Always keeping in mind natural flexion, we should start with the horse being still, and ask for a flexion of the neck.

Drawing Towards Us

Placing ourselves in front of the horse, at a distance of about three metres, we start to move to the side, towards his haunches. Should the horse move towards us, we apply a light pressure towards the part that is coming towards us, compressing the air more or less suddenly, depending on the reaction of the horse. This should be a little 'go away', not to make him yield space, but sufficient to interrupt his movement. Having reclaimed immobility, we start again.

Without the horse moving his feet (at our little 'go away!'), when we move towards his haunches, his head should follow us as if it were magnetically drawn towards us.

Lateral flexion. The horse yields laterally following the movement of the hand as if he were attracted to it.

If he doesn't do this, or at any time interrupts this following movement of the head and turns straight, we need only to click our tongue a bit, or pat a hand on our thigh to get his attention again.

Once the head has followed us towards the haunches, we should move back in front of him, with his head continuing to follow us, and try on the other side.

YIELDING OF THE HAUNCHES

Starting on the side that is easiest for him according to his natural flexion (left side for a right-flexion horse), we will try this time to move the horse's haunches towards the outside.

With the horse still, we will start by placing ourselves in front of him at about three metres away, as we would for the moving of the head. In fact we should proceed in the same way: with the horse's head following us, we should move towards the haunches, reaching the neutral point found directly behind the withers, where we should stop.

Yielding of the haunches.

At this point we will have a stationary horse who is watching us from the side. Because we want him to move his haunches, we direct our gaze and start a gentle pressure, moving our body towards them, going straight, not sideways as if we wanted to ask a forwards movement. The horse will manage to understand the difference, even though it is minimal.

Encouraging him with little clicks of our tongue, or patting our thigh with our hand, we should draw his head towards us whilst, at the same time pushing his haunches away. The horse should produce a small forward movement, with his hind legs making a wider circle than the forelegs.

With time, we should be able to slow down the forelegs until we cause the horse to make a complete rotation of his haunches around his shoulders. Be careful not to completely block the forelegs as this could be dangerous for the joints and therefore counterproductive. As always, when proceeding with the exercises, it will be our responsibility to identify critical points and to find a remedy to them. Gradually, everything will be possible. We should always have faith in ourselves and in our horse, attentively looking at every detail without losing the overall picture.

If, during our request, the horse runs off, it could mean that we have used too much pressure. it's not a problem; stop him (we should now be capable of doing it) and start again.

If he moves ahead without moving his haunches onto the outside track, it is very probable that there is not a good balance between the drawing of the head and the pushing out of the haunches.

Clearly, we do not want the horse to immediately make a complete rotation, but we absolutely must catch the first positive sign, that is, when he shows his intention of doing it. At that point we should immediately stop all pressure and give a pause of confirmation. Afterwards we should start again, trying to get a little more, but always ready to go back whenever it appears necessary.

DRAWING THE SHOULDER TOWARD US

We should start in the usual way and, as always, the same recommendations apply regarding natural flexion (left side for right-flexion horse).

We always place ourselves in front of the horse and move ourselves to the side with his head following us, this time though we stop at the level of his shoulder, a little before the withers.

We want the horse to come towards us, making a lateral step, with the shoulders (which tend to turn around the haunches) making a larger circle than that made by the haunches.

The horse looks at us and we start slowly to move back, trying to draw his front end towards us. We can reinforce our 'magnet' by gently clicking our tongue or patting our thigh with our hand whilst moving backwards. We could, if this does not suffice, move slightly towards his haunches, always gently going backwards so as to increase the drawing of his head to the side.

Drawing towards us of the shoulder with slight flexion of the neck.

As always, we should be ready to reward the horse's intention with immediate cessation of requests, or to react to possible misunderstandings, which must never place us in incorrect attitudes.

TOUCHING THE HORSE

Physical contact is admissible within the realm of possible interactions among members of a herd, such as grooming (reciprocal scratching), in the phase of nursing and, of course, for mating and naturally during conflicts for dominance. Now, the point is that we do not want to reproduce any of the above-mentioned situations. Instead, we need to touch the horse to clean him, care for him, saddle him and so on. Without any physical contact all of this would be impossible and therefore we have to try to make the horse accept a different type of relationship.

Let's summarize for a while, what has happened up until now.

Through our interaction with the horse and all the exercises conducted, we have managed to bring about some changes of state to his instinctive mode of action, which involve variants of no small importance. The first important variant brought about is that there now exists an alternative to flight and therefore this no longer possesses its initial virtue: that is, to get him out of trouble. Indeed, he has more than once experienced the futility of this attitude, which has gradually been downgraded in the scale of his instinctive reactions.

Our role is now clearer to him. He doesn't see us as a horse – he never will – but he has understood that this strange biped being has a way of behaving that's not totally inconsiderate. His actions are starting to be subordinated to ours and respect and collaboration are starting to come into the sphere of possibilities.

Let's proceed. Our frankness, an essential attitude, should never be taken for aggression, or our cautious nature for insecurity.

Let's analyse the situation before proceeding, as, at this point, we need to be very careful if we are dealing with a horse who tends to be aggressive or insecure, and we should behave accordingly.

With the horse stationary, we should put ourselves in front of him and start to get closer, always keeping an eye on his reactions and attitudes. If his state doesn't change, we can proceed. If, instead, he shows signs of restlessness, for example turning his head, we must stop and, if necessary, go back a bit. The turning of the head is, in fact, the first sign that he will take flight because he feels threatened. We should wait for a change in his state before proceeding. If, instead, he lowers his ears with the intent of biting us, showing his teeth, it is clear that he does not tolerate our presence inside his space and therefore we should give him a convincing 'go away', return to the beginning if need be and then start again (always be careful with horses who are too aggressive). Once he has restored himself to a calm and serene attitude, we should approach him up to a distance where we could easily touch his forehead with our hand.

At this point we can try to touch him, bringing our hand to his forehead.

This meeting requires reciprocal willingness, therefore we should stop our hand if the horse pulls back (doing so before this happens would be ideal), trying to maintain the same distance without retracting it. Please note: this means that if the horse begins to pull back when we are ten centimetres away, we shouldn't let it become fifteen – instead, following the horse's movement, make sure that those ten centimetres stay as such (*see* Chapter 9, Desensitization). Eight centimetres away is no good either; we must stay at ten. After this, we should wait for a change in state and hence proceed until we can place our hand on his forehead.

If, once touched, he should pull back, we should maintain the contact with the movement until he is stabilized and take it away the second he is stable and de-contracted. He will show this by lowering his head a little onto our hand with regular breathing. We should repeat this until the horse executes the whole exercise showing positive reactions.

This is the correct procedure, but it is never certain to succeed. The really important thing, however, is that at the end of the lesson the horse has a calm attitude. We should spend a bit more of our time repeating and starting again from a few steps back until this happens and, if for the moment we don't feel as if we are making progress, we should simply interrupt the exercise and have another go later on.

In the same way we should proceed to desensitize him and make him accept our touch on all the rest of his body, always taking care to remain in a position of safety and, if necessary, using a schooling whip as an extension of our hand, especially when going to touch those parts that could be dangerous for us.

We should in due course adopt the same procedure to make him accept the brush, the blanket, the numnah, the saddle and so on.

The language and therefore the grammatical structure is always the same. What will change

Backing up.

are the conditions to which we will adapt the procedures to sensitize or desensitize parts of the horse or the horse as a whole, seeking harmonious reactions.

BACKING-UP

In my opinion, during work at liberty, to teach a horse to back-up is one of the most intense and efficient exercises of all, especially so for aggressive horses, but not only them.

To back-up means to yield to a direct frontal pressure without escaping or turning, maintaining a visual contact with the source of pressure, absorbing and reacting to it, yielding space by retreating in a straight line.

This exercise is a very efficient way to re-establish dominance without losing contact, space and time, putting the horse in a receptive state and one of absolute attention, making him apt to yield to the pressure.

We must place ourselves in front of the horse about three metres from him. We must teach him to yield to a pressure, channelling the flow of energy. First of all he must de-contract his haunches, which tend to stiffen up because of the weight of the rounding of the back in this movement. We should act as if we were going to make a small, controlled aggressive action. We therefore start to compress the space between us and the horse with our wall of air that pushes towards the horse. The balance of the request, based on the reactions of the horse, will lead him to assume a behaviour susceptible to our pressure. We shouldn't pressurize him too much, giving him the time to relax the tension in his haunches and allow his back to round. If he escapes, we should re-start with changes of direction until we retake control of his immobility, and therefore start again with more caution. Another possible reaction (always a consequence of our misunderstanding) could be that he rears up because of his haunches being blocked. This behaviour is easily explained by a step-by-step analysis of the situation. We should understand the sensations that the horse is going through by his attitude. He finds himself in a situation whereby our pressure has pushed his mass onto his haunches, and if these are not ready to support the load and therefore to ease the pressure through movement, they will have the effect of a wall, off which the pressure will bounce back, amplified by the actual mass of the horse. In these conditions the horse will consequently find himself obliged to channel the flow of energy through available open doors, which will be escape: either venting the flow off sideways, or venting it off vertically (rearing).

That said, the pressure should be regulated by us so as to allow the hind legs to begin to let the energy flow through movement, with an immediate cessation of the request as soon as this happens. Through repetition of the exercise, the haunches will acquire the mobility necessary to produce a fluid movement under an increased load.

TRUST

At this point we should have acquired a good communicative ability through the exercises we have carried out, which will have established control of the horse's movements. As a consequence, our safety has increased and we can start to trust our horse. Of course, this doesn't necessarily mean that the horse will, in turn, start to trust us. Everything will depend, not on what we have done, but on how we have done it.

Up until now, we have never allowed the horse to follow us. This was intentional. We did not know with whom we were dealing and, above all, we had no control over him. And not to have control over a half-tonne being, could be quite unpleasant.

Let's teach him to come with us.

We place ourselves at the side of the horse, a little forward of his head, but before we proceed, let's take note of some rules.

The horse's head must never be ahead of us when he walks with us for the first time. In future we can adapt the position to the requirement, but not for now.

If we stop, he must stop too, adapting his movements to ours.

The distance between us and the horse must be maintained. Therefore he must not close in

When working in open spaces it can sometimes be difficult to retain the horse's attention.

or move away too much. Between half a metre and a metre and a half should be a reasonable distance within which to carry out this exercise. If the horse shows insecurity the distance can be increased. We must acquire consistency, which will be the key to open the door to trust.

So, we start by distancing ourselves from the horse, proceeding in a straight line, walking backwards in the act of drawing him towards us, stimulating him if necessary by clicking our tongue or patting our thigh with our hand. As soon as the horse starts to be drawn to us, we should stop and go to him, giving him a gentle stroke.

If the horse doesn't move, we can try with some lateral movements (which are usually very efficient), to draw him to one side and reward him as soon as he starts to move.

There may be cases in which the horse's diligence is excessive, invading our space too much in an attempt at physical contact. In such cases it will be necessary to re-establish the distance with small compressions of the wall of air, or by backing him up. The horse will immediately understand the boundaries, which he must not cross. With young stallions these boundaries must be reaffirmed often, since it is rooted in their instinct to try to overbear, dominate, subordinate, so that their genes can be passed on. Often their hormonal charge takes precedence over all their other senses, clouding their instincts and fixing them on a single goal: sex at all costs.

They can have a very high and unstable level of energy, which is often difficult and dangerous to control. Their level of energy tends to stabilize towards seven or eight years of age, and it is therefore understandable that they may be a handful before reaching a stable relationship in which the individual horse accepts his role and manages to control his instincts.

Through the correct actions, in this case close changes of direction towards the outside, the horse is brought to a correct level of attention, re-establishing leadership. Always bring the horse to a situation of serenity and trust.

Of course there are some very stable stallions, but as a rule, when we have to deal with them (which is usually the case for me), we should pay special attention to their altering changes of state, so as to interpret them in time and always be able to anticipate them. The primary characteristic required of anyone working with entire male horses is that of always 'being vigilant', and it is necessary to have a very careful control of space.

The space must be maintained even when we compress it to go in the horse's direction. For example, we can educate him in this, with wide circles keeping him to our inside, by adjusting the pressure.

Once the horse has learned to follow us in a sincere manner, we can start to turn our back on him in order that he follows us, always keeping the awareness of the space that separates us and adjusting it by actions of drawing-in or pushing away.

TEST

To assess the efficiency of our training, we can easily carry out some practical tests that will indicate where and how we should work to clarify or extend the horse's education. Let us always remember that he never lies and therefore his replies will always be honest, reflecting the reality of our way of interacting. Therefore, an assessment based on the horse's reactions will always be ruthlessly honest.

Always carefully evaluate to what extent and how the horse respects space and reacts to the compression of air mass and to attraction.

Don't touch the horse to make him execute the exercises – it is counterproductive. If we are drawing the horse towards us and, at a certain point we find him on top of us, there is something that is not working, whilst if at every tiny gesture we make, he tenses up and escapes, the concept that flight is futile has not been made sufficiently clear, or our attitude is not as coherent as we think.

In order to educate him, we must let him educate us and accept his criticism; criticism that is always constructive.

CHAPTER 16

Aggressive Horses – Let's Not Harm Ourselves!

A horse has the physical potential to hurt us. Very rarely does he also have the intention to do so. However, when these two characteristics come together, the danger can be absolutely real.

Horses can be naturally aggressive, or induced to be.

At first glance, especially if we don't know the subject's history, it is not simple to assess whether his aggression is natural or induced, whether his behaviour is rooted in defence or dominance. What we must understand is that our safety, and consequently the horse's, is at risk. It will be necessary to interact, in order to educate or re-educate the horse, taking due precautions.

Before proceeding it is necessary to understand that most aggressive attitudes are 'induced', that is, produced by humans. A horse who is uncomfortable, to whom suffering has been caused (even involuntarily) is a horse who can chose to defend himself. Suffering is not necessarily only physical. With the advent of 'audacious whisperers' suffering can also be more mental than anything else and it is the most dangerous type of suffering, the type that can take root. The 'ethological language' is a very efficient instrument of interaction and requires an adequate ethical and professional sense in the person using it. We need to know what we are doing, or at least to be aware of what we are doing. Believe me if I tell you that this is not as obvious as one might think.

The principal thing that we need for dealing with aggressive horse is a secure place. An open ring accurately cordoned off, but which leaves large visible surfaces, is ideal.

The first characteristic of an aggressive horse is that he dominates the space, and any intrusion, for him, constitutes a threat or danger.

To re-establish the parameters of safety, we must teach him to yield space without hesitation.

This requires a really convincing and motivated attitude. To hesitate or to go backwards, even by mistake, is dangerous.

The 'go away' should be applied from the outside of the ring, so that we initially have a real physical barrier between us and the horse in case of emergency.

Do not enter the ring until this concept has been made absolutely clear on repeated occasions.

The 'go away' should be applied even to the slightest attitude of dominance. If the horse puts his ears back, drive him away immediately without hesitation.

Once this concept has been made clear, so that the horse goes away without opposing every time we make the slightest gesture of aggression, then we can enter the ring.

We should never attempt this alone for the first time. It is best if there are people around ready to help us in case of need.

It has happened to me more than once that a horse opposed and responded in a very aggressive way to my attempts at dominance from outside the ring, giving no indication of yielding space. I had read books and consulted experts on this topic, but never found a satisfying explanation.

The solution fell into my hands one day when I turned out a very balanced eight-year-old stallion into a paddock fenced with electricity, where he had a gelding to his right and a three-year-old to his left.

The stallion immediately went to show aggression to the youngster in an attempt to subordinate him, and as a result the youngster went flying off, taking himself to the furthest point possible, to the evident satisfaction of the dominant male. Having done that, the stallion took himself off energetically towards the paddock of the gelding who, to my great surprise, stood still just a few centimetres from the fence without batting an eyelid. The stallion was more surprised than I was, and used all the best numbers of his repertoire; rearing and charging that would have shaken even the most fearless of hearts – he tried everything from every angle, but nothing! The gelding remained there with an arrogant air, indifferently repelling flies with his tail. He did not move away one millimetre and even less did he condescend to give the stallion a glance. I remained curious, but did not immediately make a connection (have I already mentioned how obtuse I am?) and went away. That evening, I returned to take the stallion back to his box and noticed something amazing. Even the three-year-old wasn't responding to his charges any more. Of course, he wasn't as impassive as the gelding, but even he was staying close to the fence and no longer taking himself off to the further point, much to the indignation of the stallion, who was still trying to send him away, but in an increasingly less convincing way. His failure was weakening his convictions. I began to reflect. The youngster had, in no time at all, developed an awareness of the impassability of the fence, and consequently had adapted his behaviour. Was the reverse process possible? Could a horse develop aggression if he felt sure of not having direct interaction? I wasn't convinced of it yet.

I continued for some time to put the stallion in the usual paddock and nothing more happened than previously described, except that the charges were beginning to fade more and more. Until, one day, I noticed something different. The three-year-old was replying with great intensity to the charges of the stallion, opposing them and returning the 'tit for tat', not at all intimidated. And they weren't playing either. I had to ask myself a question. If the electric fencing hadn't been there, how would things have gone? Surely not like this. The youngster would have run like hell using every breath in his body. Of this I was certain.

Therefore, this meant that my hypothesis could be correct. The horse could develop an aggressive mimicry as long as he felt protected from real interaction with his neighbour. This opened a door for me which looked out on unfamiliar horizons.

In this case, the fact that a simple electric wire can somehow provide a sense of protection and induce consequent behaviour is food for thought. One of these thoughts can be that, with an increase in the safety parameters, defence mechanisms disappear in time, leaving room for new and different mechanisms. In the example above, aggressive behaviour developed from stimuli of submission. But by changing stimuli, could we develop conditions for collaboration? And above all, could the horse's overconfidence somehow undermine ours?

Another thought could be that (again depending on the character) somehow we always need to keep in mind some small parameters of vulnerability in the horse, so that he retains his role and doesn't try to command.

Anyway, I began to see things differently and behaved according. I placed a very wide pole in the middle of the ring, so that if my convictions were proved wrong, I would nonetheless have some relative safety, using the pole to protect myself from the charges of the stallion. Interaction with (apparently) aggressive horses has happened to me many times since and I have never needed it. The pole is still there; a monument to ignorance. Mine! My theories were correct! The funny thing is that even, though the stallion responded perfectly without the barrier, once it was reinstated, he went back to his aggressive behaviour. I now knew the cause and it wasn't a problem. I still have a horse, Da Vinci di Reschio, with these characteristics. If anyone goes past or stops near his box in front of the railing, he will charge at them in a convincing manner as if he wanted to eat them. Once the door is opened, he is the most docile of horses. He is still a young stallion with all his hormones flowing, but he is a good horse; nothing to do with the 'tiger' behind the closed railing.

This is just an additional confirmation that we all come from a long road of selective evolution where only the 'strongest' survive and, that 'strongest' often means the skill of knowing how to adapt to drastic changes by developing appropriate attitudes.

A FEW THOUGHTS ON EVOLUTION

No being on earth is peaceful, and all, from bacteria up, have developed weapons of attack or defence.

Certainly, at the origins of creation that date to about four billion years and are documented by the fossil records of the earliest cellular membranes (Eubacteria and Archaebacteria, which form the family of prokaryotic cells which precede the appearance of the cellular nucleus), the concept 'I'm going to eat you' had not yet been conceived and therefore the risk of appearing on something's or some-one else's menu didn't exist. In fact the menu for these mono-cellular organisms could have been sulphur, methane and nitrogen up until the arrival of that superb invention photosynthesis, where the light supplied all the energy necessary for survival. This process of photosynthesis is the most beautiful and romantic idea of all creation; beings that are fed by light. Never mind solar panels. Not only that, but in those times of mono-cellular organisms, the concept of 'eternity' existed. The concept of growing old had not yet appeared and free radicals were unemployed.

It's the Garden of Eden, the Ediacaran period when mono-cellular organisms could grow to the considerable size of two metres, live a peaceful existence, as in 'make love not war', and would willingly have embraced each other, if only they had had arms. In reality, even the concepts of sex and war were difficult to express since they didn't yet exist. However, this is the situation described by the American geologist Mark McMenamin in his book *Garden of Ediacara*. In May 2004, the Ediacaran muscled its way into the official list of geological eras, appropriating the period between 600 million years ago and the Cambrian era of 545 million years ago. The latter, the Cambrian, is surely the most obscure and most interesting period from the point of view of changes. It is in this period in fact, that the concept of 'I'm going to eat you' was introduced. The problem is that we still don't know what the real processes were that triggered this mechanism. Unless, of course, we include magic.

However, at a certain moment – we don't know precisely either how or when – all that came to an end; the arms race started.

In August 1909 Charles Doolittle Walcott was returning from an arduous expedition of collecting fossils in the Canadian Rocky Mountains, when his horse dug his heels in at a certain point where a landslide had restricted the path.

The obstinate animal just refused to go forward. So Walcott, no longer a youngster, dismounted intending to patiently remove some of the rocks to allow his stubborn horse to pass more easily, even though he could have got through anyway. And so it was, that whilst moving the fallen debris, his eyes fell on a slab of shale where lay the curled up fossil of something that, up to that time, even our most bizarre fantasies could not have imagined. It was the *Marrella splendens*, a species of (armoured) crab with horns, legs and various other things.

Subsequently at that site (Burgess Shale) more than one hundred species came to light with the discovery of more than 65,000 fossils armed with weapons of mass destruction dating back to the Cambrian era, about 500 million years ago. Thanks to a stubborn horse.

The explosion of the Cambrian era, as it is defined by geologists, is the one that definitely proclaimed the dictats of an evolutionary competitive change where existence for its own sake was no longer possible. One could no longer float on the water's surface lulled by placid sea currents and fed by light. Why? Simply because, from then, on one was part of something more complex, but most of all, one was part of the menu.

From this event, a theory has been formed that is largely shared by many scholars and which I will try to summarize.

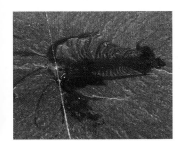

Marrella splendens.

Starting from the principle that certain conditions exist in which life can develop and therefore evolve, it will always do so by first taking into account primary resources. If there were an abundance of a particular element, life would develop on the basis of this. If, all other conditions being equal, there was an abundance of nitrogen, life would develop on that basis. The same would apply to oxygen or other elements, strongly reaffirming the concept of opportunity. Now, since apparently in the Ediacaran era there was an abundance of peaceful beings all crammed together, the appearance of a being who could somehow exploit such resources (concept of opportunity) could have been a consequence of this, much as the extermination of these defenceless creatures would itself become a consequence. Therefore, the need for defences, which up until then had not been necessary, now triggered an exponential race toward change. This, among other things, would also lead to the invention of symmetry resulting from movement intended as a weapon of defence or attack.

Up until then in fact, the concept of mobility wasn't really necessary to life. What managed to evolve? Only those beings who adopted efficient strategies, who managed in some way to survive and consequently to transmit their genes and who adopted flight as a defence mechanism. (Obviously only those who had legs, or a tail, or … something useful for escaping from someone other than using the mouth … somebody that, on the other side, had to move if he wanted to eat). The others, among them a great number of 'armoured' beings, can be considered as failed attempts.

And indeed we can affirm without a shadow of a doubt that there were many more failures than evolutionary successes, including those caused by external events such as meteorites, climate changes and so on. However, some of us, starting from a common root and then

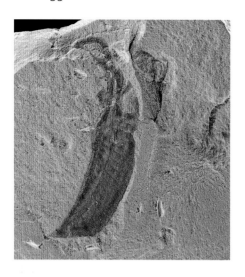

diversifying, have managed to make it right up to today. It appears that this common root was a small creature, the Haikouella, in the shape of a sausage, whose photo we should all have in our family album as our first real ancestor.

The story goes on … in the sense that the evolutionary process is still continuing. We are not in a finite period; many species are being stamped out right now, while you are reading, whilst others are changing. It is only thanks to study and certainly not to our inadequate concept of time, that we can, with difficulty, be aware of it.

Photo of the original ancestor 'HAIKO' (Haikouella).

CHAPTER 17

The Modulation of Pressures

Pressures are the linguistic base through which horses express themselves. The modulation of pressures is its grammatical implementation. The grammatical understanding of a language becomes all the more complex, and therefore subject to interpretation, the fewer the words that form it. In the case of the language of the horse, words can be substituted by pressure, which, like a Japanese ideogram, will express the concept but not its objective. A concept could for example, express doing something, but not what, how or when. Take the root of a verb, for example, the verb 'to do'. In itself, it may not mean much, whereas 'I have done my homework' already expresses something different. This concept, however, will remain an end in itself without the expression of intentions. Intentions can be communicated only by using other factors:

- Space
- Direction
- Time
- Intensity

Which, in turn, trigger reactions, upon which we should modulate the pressures themselves and the variables described above.

As we have already seen, it is not just 'pushing' pressures that exist. In order to draw-in a horse and make him come towards us for example, there is an 'attracting' pressure, the existence of which is based on the existence of the positive or 'pushing' pressure. Just as the proton and the electron are equal in intensity but have opposite charges, the pressures of pushing or attracting can be seen in the same way, consequently modulated and then expressed.

For example, in a de-contracted horse, who is well educated and receptive to communication, moving the point of contact further forward, lengthening the reins, will produce an extension of the neck, caused by a 'pulling' pressure and not by a loss of the contact of our hands with him. So long as the horse has a good education, and the contact is moved within the physical limits of the horse (he can reach it) it will lead him to what he is looking for, a comfortable condition.

The confirmation of our intentions and therefore their correct interpretation by the horse will be given to us only by his reactions, which in turn will require a counter-reaction on our part, to confirm whether or not his interpretation of this intention is correct. Therefore, by the intention, we will create an association of intent. That is to say, we can't leave the horse a 'PS' with a list of things he has to do and expect that, once he has read it, he will do them. We need to request, be sure that he has done it and then, most importantly, confirm to him that what he is doing or has just done is right.

- *'Excuse me, could you move over a bit'* – Intention.
- *'What?'* – Reaction.
- *'No, to the other side please'* – Negative counter-reaction (the request continues, and its intensity can change, but not the intention).
- *'Is that better?'* – Reaction.
- *'Perfect, thank you'* – positive counter-reaction, sensitive lessening or immediate interruption of the request.

Everything needs to be modulated, that is, adapted from moment to moment. So a request, executed by a pressure (whether positive or negative) is composed of the following variables:

- Direction
- Space
- Time
- Intensity

These should be expressed as a complex action regulated by their modulation.

If this were not done – if we used the same expressive intensity for each variable– the grammatical form would become flat and lose its communicative capacity.

We need to establish some rules to which we should refer every time we realize that the results have gone out of control.

One of these is surely intensity, the weapon of the poet. Let's proceed with this concept, always bearing in mind that I am seeking to encode in writing, a bodily communicative form. I can describe to you a photograph and seek to re-create a similar image by describing it and what it contains, but I will never manage to transmit the exact image to your mind.

Intensity is the essence of expression. We can liken it to the volume of the television. This has to be regulated so it can be understood. My son's baby-sitter has the television on really loud and it's not that she can't hear; it's just a habit. Many people, when they are discussing something and are not in agreement, tend to raise their voices, quickly finding themselves shouting, trying to give a greater emphasis to their reasoning. The problem is that this often triggers a situation in which everyone is shouting but no one remembers why. It's a bit like the joke of the ant who, by chance, fell on the back of a charging elephant who destroyed everything in his path. When another ant asked him what he was doing up there he replied with emphasis: 'I don't know what I was doing, but we were making one hell of a mess!'

Now, what could the right parameter of body language be, through which to modulate the intensity?

I strongly hope that you can reply after all that you have read.

The reply is the awareness of being felt. Awareness understood as being aware. Take great care that this does not mean 'the certainty of having a reply' – absolutely not, in that this could depend on other factors; for example the horse's decision to ignore our request. Why? Because he can. It's simply possible.

Here we are speaking of something different, of the ability to understand, of being felt, and not that of being heard. These are two different things. It should be on the basis of the former (the certainty of being felt) that the intensity of our interactions and therefore our requests should normally be measured.

We have at our disposal all the factors for this to happen. We have 'only' to learn to recognize them, to believe them and to carry them out.

If we start with the assumption that the horse is not responding to us because he can't feel us, the outcome will be inevitably be that of finding ourselves shouting against the wind, gradually increasing the intensity of our actions, achieving, to all intent, a gradual desensitization.

If, on the other hand, we start with the concept of being felt, but not being listened to, we should make modulated actions like, for example, a small aggressive action, to restore the correct level of attention. Easy choices do not exist, but consistent choices do. Through the modulation of pressure, either that of pushing or drawing, we can take our interaction to a higher and more personalized level.

To express myself in a better way, we can calmly take all the rules we have read up until now and throw them in the wastepaper basket. You read correctly. Provided, however, that we have managed to achieve such an extent of collusion that they are no longer needed. I mean to say that, if we manage to express ourselves on a level that isn't grammatical but energetic (understand well that I don't mean transcendental), then it is possible.

The sensory abilities of the horse are as yet unexplored, so don't be surprised if you obtain a response to the intention of your request, if you can recognize and reward the intention of the response.

The link, the collaboration, the interaction and the understanding will all reinforce themselves with time and, if the process is carried out well, we will be able to refine it to a point that will enable us (both us and our horse) to do wonderful things. It will only depend on us to establish its limits. I feel I should give a word of advice, to spend as much time as possible together with your horse, without doing anything. Be with him whilst he grazes for as many hours as possible, with an open mind and be ready to receive without asking. I assure you that with time many questions will find answers – answers that you will never find written in a book. Always watch out for those who claim to teach techniques that are too transcendental. They will teach us a technique that will perhaps help us to reach a deeper awareness of ourselves, but they should not manipulate us in any way. Moreover, any technique that we try to learn should have our safety as its prime objective. Only thus, feeling ourselves understood, can we then respect and understand others. Excuse the petty philosophy but I believe that, at this point of the book, it can at least be tolerated.

Clearly this is possible and welcomed, but surely only obtained over time and through experience, that is, after following a route based on certain rules that we should hold on to and return to every time we get lost.

Therefore, let's retrieve our rules from the waste-paper basket and try to follow them.

DIRECTION

The direction towards which we employ a pressure, whether it is drawing or pushing, has the primary function of expressing intent.

There isn't much more to say, except that direction should be modulated just as intensity and, like it, can therefore be used to reinforce intention. The direction of pressure, just like intensity, should always adhere to the principle of lightness and return to it after every act of reinforcing intent. We must return to the awareness of being felt.

SPACE

This also can be modulated, and must be carried out with the same principles as direction and intensity.

TIME

Time is not an element that uses the principles of modulation. It is the very grammatical structure on which all the other principles are based.

Time is linked to body language like sound or, better modulated to the word and as such, is what allows the bodily expression to take on meaning. Time is the rule. It has very precise parameters and the more these are respected the clearer the result will be. It is subdivided into moments of intent and every action, protracted or interrupted moment-by-moment, (that is, a moment before or a moment after), will determine its meaning.

So, to see time as something that can be modulated because it varies is a mistake. The varying of time is its very essence; essence from which modulation draws its roots. Never the opposite.

Time does not regulate pressure, but it determines its duration and therefore its meaning. Intensity, just as space and direction, must be modulated to show its intent.

Let's summarize:

- Direction – determines intention
- Space – is a reinforcement
- Intensity – is how much

And all of them can be modulated, whilst:

- Time – determines the meaning

Logically one would think that it is 'time' that determines 'how long' and not 'intensity'. But if we have begun to understand body language, it shouldn't be difficult for us, at this point, to understand why this is so. If not, it means that we have missed something and we should go back to understand better.

Otherwise, let's go on.

The more we manage to modulate our exercises, the more the parameters of lightness will be maintained. What we do with the horse should acquire an element of fluidity, which is a characteristic of correct modulation. If, instead, the horse replies to us like a lamp with the switch going 'on-off …' we are not there yet.

Our objective shouldn't be that of doing something, but of doing it well. If we ask our horse to go into a canter and to get this result we have to run behind him, it's not working. If, in order to effect a transition to halt, we have to cut off his route every time, it means that our language is not yet formed properly and we are expressing ourselves like a kerbstone.

If we want to improve, we need to 'get' the horse's intention to do. It requires patience, understanding but most of all, temerity. We must demand more of ourselves; the horse has been ready to give us more for a long time. This is also because, for the horse, from a communicative point of view, more means better and for him, as for us, there is always room for better.

CHAPTER 18

Interaction with the Headcollar

This time we will use a headcollar and a lead rope, but note that the concepts we learned during work at liberty remain the same. We should not use the lead rein to pull the horse or to hold him back, but only educate him to it in such a way that he may learn its properties – properties that we must be the first to respect.

The properties of the lead rope and the headcollar that we want the horse to learn are those that reproduce the communicative aspects of the reaction of the mounted horse. Not *only* those to be precise, but they will be the majority.

One of these aspects is direct pressure or contact pressure.

Even the concept of contact will change in direct or physical contact, becoming palpable (it has always been tangible).

As with direct contact, direct pressure will not be exempt from grammatical forms, which will largely reflect those seen so far with work at liberty.

Direct contact does not need modulation, it is finite. It is the certainty of feeling by touch and of being felt. If it is stronger it becomes an involuntary pressure, which is the main cause of suffering and misunderstanding between horse and rider. If it is too weak, it simply ceases to exist.

It is easy to understand and implement in a static situation, much less so in a dynamic one. This is one of the reasons why I do not recommend the continuation of work on the ground in movement. It is obvious that its execution will be complex because of poor contact caused by the differences in locomotion between human and horse. To work a horse on long-reins is very highly complex. It is crazy to pretend that a young trainer can do it, especially with a young horse. Also, I have to add, this work is often done directly on the bit ….

I have often seen inexperienced people 'working' their horses on various forms of 'long-reins' in strange and unusual ways (knots, crossed reins, various pulleys, and so on), arguing it was too early to saddle them. Many times, people do not have sufficient awareness of what they are doing ….

All work on the ground can be carried out without direct contact and so I see neither use nor reason for it. Lungeing the horse is different because the distance and the weight of the lunge line can emulate a direct contact, disguising the difference in speed between human and horse. We will look at this further on.

Before starting we must be sure that we have understood the most important aspect of contact, which is stability. The stability of contact should never be confused with being static. In order for the contact to be stable, it must move with the horse, following him without opposing him. It must always be the same and maintained over time. Therefore it is not static.

We will need a long rope, which should be concentrically rolled up in our hand, starting with large coils that get smaller. This is because, if the horse escapes for whatever reason, we will have the means of allowing his movements without getting caught up in the rope, and having the largest coil last will give us a greater margin of time before it all unravels. It seems trivial, but we should always keep our rope in an orderly fashion.

The headcollar should always be simple and comfortable, like those used in the paddock, so to speak, with three rings, one each side and the other underneath.

LATERAL YIELDING OF THE NECK

Placing ourselves to the side of the horse, immediately behind the withers, we hook the rope on the inside side ring of the headcollar. Our objective will be to make the horse execute pronounced flexions of the neck towards the inside, to teach him to yield to pressure from the rope.

The first thing we should do is to establish contact between our hand and the headcollar through the rope to the outside part of the horse's muzzle. This is because it is here that we are going to apply pressure. For us it will be a pulling action, whilst for the horse it will be pushing one, in that the pulling pressure on the internal ring will in fact have a pushing action on the external part of the muzzle.

Once contact is established, we begin to apply a small pressure, which should be interrupted (yielding) at every sign of flexion, re-establishing a contact. The correct sequence is always the same: don't lose the contact during the yielding phase. However, we take care as it will be initially be difficult for us to do this successfully. My suggestion is to focus on the right moment in which to yield. Conversely, if the horse does not yield to the pressure, modulate the same by intensifying it.

Internal flexion.

External flexion.

We must, however, absolutely avoid creating an induced leaning on the contact. If we manage to modulate the pressure well and release it when the horse begins yielding, re-establishing a contact, this should not happen. Tact is required to anticipate a positive reaction. Once the intent has been established, we should manage, through modulation, adopting the concept of 1+1, to attain an even deeper flexion from even lighter requests.

We shouldn't be satisfied with our training until the horse also follows our hand in the other direction, that is bringing himself to an extended position, always maintaining contact or, even better, moving it forward so that he is induced to seek it. Initially, to obtain this response, we can slacken the rope slightly. If we conduct our work well, in a short time the horse will flex and extend his neck, following the movement of our hand rather than the pressure, reducing contact to little more that the weight of the rope itself. The proof will be in carrying out this exercise without the rope, just with the movement of our hand.

Once this is done on both sides, dedicating more time to the side where flexion is not natural, we carry out the exercise by changing the ring to which the rope is attached from the inside to the outside and letting the rope pass behind the horse's neck. We do this on both sides. This means we will ask for a right flexion whilst remaining on the left side and vice versa.

EXTENSION OF THE NECK AND VERTICAL FLEXION

We hook the rope to the ring which is underneath the headcollar, positioning ourselves in front of the shoulder, about halfway along the neck.

This time we will use our left hand on the horse's left side and right hand on his right side.

We should start by placing our hand gently on the horse's muzzle at the level of the clip of the rope only above, on the other side, i.e. on the point where the horse will receive the pressure when it is applied with the rope. We establish the contact, and commit to maintaining it even if the horse moves his head, by following his movements with our hand. We start to impart gentle pressure, not pushing, but gently rolling our hand around his muzzle and gently squeezing. By modulating the pressure we will obtain reactions. Now, as always, we should identify the one we are looking for, which is for the horse to start to bring his head down and forwards. Clearly we are not concerned with other reactions and therefore, even if the horse tries to escape or resist the pressure, we should keep it. Note, that maintaining the pressure doesn't mean increasing or decreasing it, even if the horse's head moves. The moment the

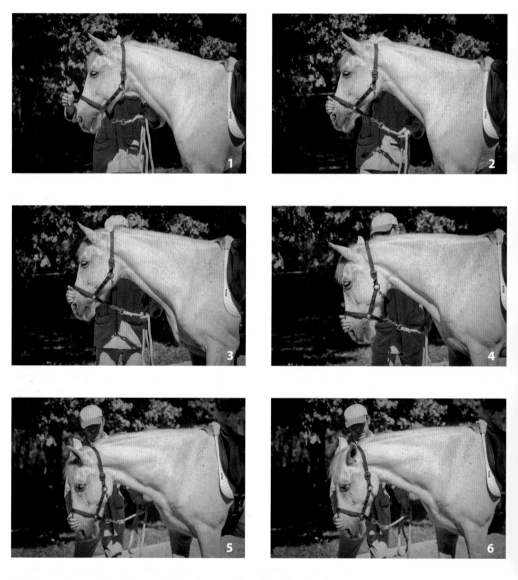

Yielding and extension with association between hand and head collar.

horse starts to show a reaction in the direction we want, our pressure should be interrupted, quickly passing to contact. It is always the same; we always use the same methodology, only this time, we will use our hand. This way we will understand the difficulty of maintaining a contact and a pressure that accommodates the movements and reactions of the horse more directly. At the start it can seem complex, especially if it is the first time that we have carried out a similar exercise, but it is important to understand and learn to accommodate the movements of the horse without losing contact, maintaining a constant intensity of pressure.

We should arm ourselves with patience and continue until the horse accommodates our pressure, seeking our contact as a positive and desirable thing. The object will be to induce him to lower his head, de-contracting his muscles, making a small rotation of the cervical vertebrae, tending to bring his forehead onto the vertical, with an extension of his neck on a level with his back. Believe me that this is not an uncomfortable position for the horse, indeed it's a position of relaxation that he will learn to appreciate once he has understood.

We have two huge advantages in carrying out this exercise in correct way. The first is in understanding in a direct way how to maintain contact and pressure whilst accommodating the horse's movements. The second, should the horse be over-excited, is having control of making him assume a physical position of relaxation – one that can considerably influence him in regaining calmness through precisely the position itself. This refers to the concept we have seen before, that the mind and body of the horse are linked, and therefore, if we make an excited horse assume a relaxed position this will have a direct effect on his attitude.

Remember? Things are what they appear. And also: Change the appearance ,you change the essence.

When we are able to make the horse execute this exercise calmly, without opposition and more importantly with lightness, we start to substitute the pressure from our hand with that of the headcollar through the rope, initially ready to intervene with the hand in case of misunderstanding. If we summarize this situation, we see that in this phase we already have control of the horse's neck in static form (from standstill) through direct pressure, with lateral and vertical yielding and extensions. Even the concept of direct contact has been laid down.

Many people would now start to teach the horse to back-up through pressure of the rope. I don't do this and I advise you not to either. The risk is that the horse will move himself backwards, confusing this with pressure to yield his neck. Our horse already knows how to back-up; we have done this exercise in work at liberty. If need be, we can repeat the same procedure using body language rather than with pressure from the rope. More importantly, the first time we mount the horse, it will be fundamental that he goes forwards rather than backwards in order to avoid him forming any possible defences. We will have plenty of time to teach him to go backwards under saddle.

Let's always remember that the horse won't do what he doesn't know, and it's best if, when we mount him for the first time, he knows only a few essential and concrete things.

One of these things, as essential as the 'go away' in work at liberty, is for him to take himself forward at the slightest request.

A PAUSE FOR THOUGHT

Horses can change their attitudes in an instant and this instant of change is never a pretence but always real and sincere. We, on the other hand, even if we tried with our best intentions, would always struggle to make every moment of change real and sincere. Only by producing

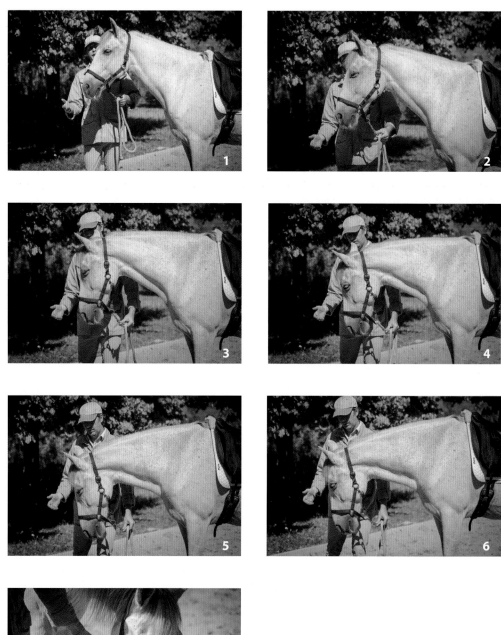

Yielding and extension only with the head collar.

a 'clean' thought, (one free of any contamination that might impede our intention to reflect it) will we be able to feel really in tune with a being who lives outside falsehood.

The need that sometimes leads us to deceive others – that of always trying to live beyond what we really are – often serves only to deceive ourselves, making us miss the real picture, for fear of not being accepted, or not being 'up to the task'. Horses show themselves for what they are, and have often forced me, personally, to find a less blurred vision of my identity, which I didn't like seeing. When we have a relationship with a horse, or with animals in general, we usually don't feel the need to show ourselves as anything other than what we are, because we feel that they accept us anyway and moreover don't judge us. With time therefore, our true 'I' will find a way of showing itself in a more natural way than it does in interaction with our own kind. Being more sincere will help to avoid misunderstandings and make communication more fluid and grammatically correct.

In all this wonderful stuff, there is a something especially worthy of reflection. Lying, for us, is a natural thing and an integral part of the human being. It is part of our evolutionary journey. It has nothing to do with sin or right and wrong. If we look at the concept from an anthropological point of view (with a more scientific approach), putting aside for a second our socio-cultural heritage, we can see the subject in a different light.

Recent studies have shown that to lie, in particular, to lie to ourselves, is nothing more than a self-defence mechanism that often helps us during certain phases of our lives. I am not, of course, speaking of pathological cases, or pre-meditated deceit to make a profit – they are different. I am speaking of the way that our brain changes reality in order to make us believe more in ourselves, to help us overcome obstacles that seem too difficult, or to protect us from

Francesco Busignani (student instructor FEEL).

them. I am speaking of a kind of hope where believing is therapeutic in many situations. The famous saying 'look at the glass as being half full rather than half empty' is none other than a positive interpretation of reality. Not only this, but the ability to lie is a function of an evolved mind.

It goes without saying, that an evolved mind that can consider a lie as a possibility also has the ability to assess the truth and can therefore defend itself so that the fight is balanced. For a simpler mind, things change radically. In fact let's not continue to speak of lying, but of confusing appearance, trying to hide what one is, while keeping one's own identity. The mimicry used by a leopard, by a crocodile silently semi-submerged, by a lion flattened out in the savannah (or by a crevasse covered with grass), by a hidden snake and suchlike; all of these things have taught us that ambiguity often conceals danger. But they are also a mechanism of defence and survival. This is the reason why 'truthfulness', the clarity of things, is synonymous with certainty, security, stability and, the more our condition becomes uncertain, the more we yearn for these concepts. At least in theory, because in practice, for us, it doesn't work like that. Our brain can make us see things differently: depending on the genetic priorities of our spirit of conservation, it may tend to aggravate or diminish the problem. Some individuals pay to be able to go parachuting; others would not do it even under torture. Why? And the same people who go parachuting may faint at the mere sight of a hypodermic syringe. Why?

It is all part of our heritage, of the genes, of lived experience. Especially in early years of life, education, culture and chance can direct our character in a certain direction. The same is true of horses. Every individual has different characteristics; every individual contains within himself a much larger world than we often imagine. This means that nature, amongst its many attempts, admits both liberals and conservatives – the two sides of the same coin.

In conclusion, the interesting thing for us is to understand that the horse is a being who doesn't use mechanisms of mimicry for self-defence and is therefore never 'deceitful', but he knows of them, having suffered their consequences. He knows the evil, but never practises it. He is what he seems, but all the rest is not. But let's not make a saint of him… perhaps he doesn't deceive simply because he can't do it, because he is made that way…. I don't know precisely, in the same way that I don't know many things about myself. But of one thing I am certain, of all the beings on this earth; the horse is a beautiful creature. And for this I am grateful.

Coherence and always keeping a clear and transparent attitude, is the right path for a journey of trust. Falsehood is part of us; to know it is to be aware of it, so that we can better manage our reactions without condemning them.

FORWARDS

I have already said and repeated more than once that immobility is the agony of equitation. To advance, to take oneself forward, is its essence, the key that will open all the doors for us.

To respect the horse, we need to understand the use of the schooling whip, which must be considered as the extension of our hand. We can also do it without, but to avoid the risk of confusion, the schooling whip is, in this case, the most suitable instrument.

The taking himself forwards, like the 'go away', must be clear and unequivocal to the horse. Clearly, we must always be mindful of the character that distinguishes every horse as being unique and variable, adapting our interaction accordingly. This being so, we will consider some assumptions that we will then adapt as required. The dynamism, and thus the ability to vary our attitudes, will always remain an essential part of the understanding.

First, however, I must say a few important words, a necessary confession as I don the robes of the defender of good intentions.

I could affirm that, in my experience with horses, I have always respected and understood them and that I never, ever, used the whip in a violent manner....

Oh yes, I could and would dearly love to say that, but it would not be the truth and since, up to now, we have spoken of sincerity and coherence..... No, reality is quite different; I have used the whip in a violent manner. I did so to force results, with 'the best intentions', never out of sheer violence but rather out of ignorance. I did it. I seek no justifications as there are none and I write this because I believe that the errors I have committed could help others follow different paths. The use of the whip in a violent manner brought me nothing good and has always left behind it a trail of bad situations and sensations. Misunderstanding, fear, mistrust, stress.... The list would be endless. All this goes well beyond ethics; it is a situation of conscience and responsibility.

You know that little voice we hear inside us when we are doing something wrong? Well, that little voice has never abandoned me and has pushed me to take a good look around me and to look for something beyond the gratification of a sporting result, a result that is empty if it is merely an end in itself. There can always be innumerable factors that lead us to use violence in the illusory belief of finding a shorter route but, believe me, that route leads nowhere. If a relationship based on trust is what we are looking for, hitting a horse, whatever the motivations, is not the way. Every time we raise our hand to strike with the intent of obtaining something, we can be sure it is not the way to obtain it. There are different paths to follow together with horses and every one will be all the better and more gratifying the less it involves violence There are wonderful and surprising things one can do by simply enriching one's culture and every hour spent studying and dedicated to understanding will be rewarded by tranquil and restoring sleep without interruption from a niggling conscience. Trust me, it's no small thing. If, as a young man, I had been given the choice between two paths to follow, one leading towards the gratification of the result and the other towards a rapport, a better relationship with horses, I would not have had the slightest doubt which one to take. Luckily, however, things in life can change and offer us a second chance.

Let's come back to the use of the whip to take the horse forward, remaining on the ground in this case.

The principle is the same as the lesson to move off the leg on the mounted horse, which is as follows. Having educated the horse by means of vocal associations, which he knows, and by means of a light pressure of the legs repeated twice, to take himself forward, if he doesn't respond by quickly taking himself forwards, after repeating the request (we should always give him the benefit of the doubt),we maintain it and apply the schooling whip to his flanks, in an increasingly lively way until we obtain more than the reaction we require (the horse shoots forwards). 'Increasingly lively' does not mean to hit or whip the horse, but to cause surprise and a degree of discomfort, making him escape forwards. After which we should immediately cease the requests, returning the horse to walk and stroking him, and then try again. Usually, if it is done well, we should only need to carry out one or two lessons to move off the leg in the life of the horse. If we were able to master the whip, it would be sufficient to use it without actually touching the horse, rather moving it energetically near him, brushing by him. Since doing this requires a very energetic action (the whip must lash the air and only the air), there is a serious risk of hitting the horse, who would be hit quite hard if our aim were less than perfect. Hence we should be careful that, in the intention of not touching him, we don't actually achieve the opposite. Sometimes it is better to touch lightly, suddenly and with increasing intensity to keep our action and its intensity under control.

Let's now see how to carry out this lesson from the ground.

First of all we should position ourselves at the side of the horse at the level of his shoulder, holding the rope in one hand and the schooling whip in the other.

Our objective in this case will be that of sensitizing the response of the horse to the voice.

- By clicking the tongue, we ask the horse to quickly take himself forwards (if this happens in every phase of the exercise we interrupt and profusely caress the horse and then repeat, otherwise we proceed to the next point).
- We raise the schooling whip towards the haunches, continuing to ask with the voice.
- We touch the haunches with the schooling whip in a repetitive and increasing manner, still continuing to ask with the voice in order to create an association.
- We bring the horse back to a calm state and make much of him.

In repeating the exercise, it should suffice to stop at the first phase without the need to carry on to the next phase.

If, instead, the horse is restless from the first moment, we should proceed to desensitize him until we get responses consistent with our requests.

VOCAL ASSOCIATION

Because, once we are in the saddle, the horse will not be able to see us, a channel of communication, the visual one, will go missing and we will have to use hearing, which will help us transmit our intentions.

All that we have done so far and are going to do, should be associated with a verbal language. It is a simple language, learned by association, using deep tones for 'downwards' actions, for example, transitions from trot to walk or from walk to halt, and sharp tones for increasing actions.

It is of no importance which words we use; it is the intonation that counts. Clearly there are some words in our more vocal language that lend themselves better to one or the other of the aims. The vocals 'OOOoooaaaa', for example, lend themselves to the deep tones, whilst 'HIIIE' do to the sharp ones. We can also use the words that refer to a specific gait, like 'walk', 'trot', 'canter'. However, what matters is to always repeat the same thing and, more importantly, the intonation that we give the words. For example, ' waa-aalk' or 'WALK!' will have two different meanings; the first one tending to calm or slow down and the second to increase.

To create an association between body language and vocal language is fairly easy and intuitive. That is, provided that we maintain an attitude which induces the horse to respond and not to be laid-back to the request. A verbal request must always be commanding and our body must always be ready to intervene up to the level of aggression if we note that the response is not consistent or ready.

The process of training is the same:

- Vocal request
- Vocal and body request
- Vocal request and 'aggression'

And so the horse will create associations, learning to react promptly to verbal indications.

When our horse responds to the 'indications', whether these are vocal or direct, and no longer to the request, this will mean that we have achieved the most coveted goal, collaboration.

Always remember that the horse is never directly responsible for his non-collaboration; it depends on us. If our attitude is correct and consistent we can always count on him.

When we try to achieve something, our gestures, our actions must be aimed more at wooing, at inviting him, motivating the horse to collaborate without obliging him to do so. For a man it's a bit like inviting a woman to dinner, taking her flowers, convincing her with sweet nothings – naturally being aware that it will, however, be she who decides whether or not to accept our company (the result often being loneliness and a large bill). We know perfectly well what the aim of our actions is, from the dinner, the flowers and so on, so perhaps it would be more logical to say explicitly, 'Look here, my dear, let's skip all this and go directly to the finale, which is what I'm interested in.' But this would be disrespectful and maybe a bit brutal. And so the game of courtship, instead, is needed to perform all this in a way which, though less direct, is nonetheless explicit.

This is not an easy balance to reach: 'Explicit in intention, but not brutal in fact'. From the woman's point of view, I don't know what example to make, but I'm sure female readers won't struggle much to find a fitting one.

WORK ON THE LUNGE LINE

Take good note: to lunge the horse doesn't ever mean to make him jump about for us until he's tired. For this, in due time, we can leave him free without interacting with him. All horses need moments when they can vent off energy or do whatever they want to do, and ensuring that they can is part of taking care of them. So do not neglect this aspect.

Therefore we should start with a very clear idea of what we are going to do. Transitions in all three gaits without a change of rein, immobility, halt. All with the association of vocal requests.

We have previously taught the horse lateral yielding of the neck; this element will be the basis of interaction which we will perform ' in hand' on the lead rein.

Whilst we perform our actions from the ground, we should always relate ourselves to this element (in hand on the lead rein) as if we were in the saddle. Even if this may seem easier than to work in the saddle, in reality it isn't. There are, in fact, some elements that make having a good contact a bit complicated:

- The distance
- The difference in the gaits
- The weight of the lunge line
- The sudden change of space between us and the horse

These elements are discordant with implementing a good contact and, in light of this, to do so by hooking the rope directly onto the horse's mouth would be highly detrimental and counterproductive.

The promotion of such a practice (the rope attached to the mouth even by passing it through the inner ring and then over the horse's head and hooking it to the outer ring) is harmful, totally ignores the sensitivity of the horse, and causes unnecessary and preventable suffering for the sake of de-contractive gymnastics, which is inefficient.

We can easily do this later, after mounting the horse and maintaining an efficient communication. To think of doing it from the ground because we are not capable of doing it from saddle just means that we are conceited and, above all, that we have no conception of the horse. It's not like throwing a lifebuoy to someone who is drowning because we will not be able to save him, as many promoters of this system argue. Rather, it is to try to save him by throwing him a steam iron. This is the use that the horse gets out of it and it teaches nothing to those who carry it out.

The ring is not an ideal place in which to lunge the horse; a large sand school is better. I normally never use a ring (not even for work at liberty). I know perfectly well that this goes against what I have said up until now. But it is now time to understand that all that helps us initially can be counterproductive in the long run. So why did I advise you to use one? For reasons of safety and because, initially, there are many things to understand and managing the work at liberty in an undefined space can become very costly in terms of energy and time and, consequently, counterproductive in our training. If we commit an error in the ring, the horse cannot go too far away, giving us time to reflect without the additional worry of losing the trust of the horse or losing the horse himself. In a sense, if we err, we lose the trust of the horse anyway, but it will be much easier to regain it if we have the horse close to us, and he will allow us to see our mistakes more easily and understand how to modify our attitude in a more direct way and at closer intervals. It's a fair price to pay to be able to learn. There are different methods that are applied to work at liberty, but they require a very long journey, deep understanding of the interaction of the language of the herd and, most of all, sensitivity and a way of relating that can be quite complex. I am convinced that this is a milestone that each of us can reach and that would, indeed, be desirable. But the time and dedication required are substantial and absolute. Because of this I have deliberately chosen to propose a system that takes into consideration the average time that a person who is not a professional trainer will have available for working with their horse, in order to respect him and interact with him in an efficient and safe way.

First, we should pay attention to the lateral yielding that the horse will execute in answer to our pressure on the headcollar. This pressure could also come about for reasons not directly linked to our attitude, but simply because the horse is not yet educated enough to respect the circle in an undefined space. It can often happen that he tends to make the circle smaller or larger depending on where, according to him, the most comfortable place is, or if there are other horses or distractions nearby. Our hand, our arm and all of our body must be ready to maintain a dynamic contact and, through dynamism, make it constant, accommodating the movement of the horse. We yield every time the horse gives to our request and maintain the pressure, accommodating the movement, when he doesn't. This means that if our pressure on the lunge line makes the horse flex his neck a little, or if, by yielding, the space that separates us diminishes, this is a positive response and should be confirmed every time with a positive counter-reaction (yielding of the pressure). If, on the other hand, he opposes us by stiffening up or tries to increase the space (by enlarging the circle), the pressure should be maintained or reinforced until he changes his condition. The horse will soon learn to respect the lunge line, provided that we see it as an instrument through which to communicate and not as a useful object to restrain him.

If the pressure becomes too strong, it means that we have not paid attention to the yielding of the horse by not accommodating him. We try again, with more attention, the hold on the rope must just support the rope itself, creating an arc from our hand to the ring on the inside of the headcollar, keeping it a good distance from the ground. If the line goes tense, the horse must yield, modifying his state, and then consequently so must we. If he runs off and

Transition walk halt walk trot. Please note that all body movements photographed in the book are much more accentuated than is necessary. This has been done so as to make them more evident. In reality, all this abundance in requests is often too accentuated for the horse.

the pressure intensifies too much, it will become counterproductive, triggering an instinctive defence action. We must therefore accommodate the flight movements in a way whereby we maintain an efficient and constant pressure until the horse changes, yielding to the same. This, at times, can mean that we will have to run with him, making the circle bigger. If the horse, in flight, manages to go straight in his movement, all our attempts to hold him will be in vain. It is then worth letting him go and trying again, seeking to anticipate his flight with a circular movement controlled through a flexion of the neck. If the horse makes the circle too small, we can use the lunge line like a wave, produced by a rapid and circular movement of our hand, so as to induce him to enlarge the circle and restore contact. Of course we can also use our body, with an attitude of pressure towards his withers or shoulder.

Once we have obtained regular circles, with a good contact and with good yielding, we should verify what we have learned by inviting the horse to make the circle smaller with a light, attracting pressure on the line, and widening it when gently releasing the rope, inviting the horse to seek the contact.

Having done this, we can move away from the circles, and try to make the horse travel straight for a short distance, running next to him, maintaining a neutral position. If the horse shows signs of restlessness, tries to run off in any case, or increases the gait, we should be ready to bring him back to a circle in order to try again, until we can run together with him in a straight line without problems and maintain the gait. Lungeing the horse continuously on a circle serves no purpose. To interact with him, bringing changes of state, maintaining a good contact, on the other hand, helps us to understand and be understood.

Bearing in mind what I have said about the process overall, we should start by placing ourselves at the side of the horse at the level of the withers, establishing a contact through the lunge line, which should never be tense. I repeat that the weight of the line is sufficient. Having done this, we should ask for a forward movement using our voice and our body as previously described. Once we have achieved the three gaits satisfactorily, both on a circle and in a straight line, we should ask him to halt and we should prepare to change the rein. We cannot change the rein directly as we need to invert the position of the clip of the line onto the headcollar. But it's worth doing, as all of this will be useful to us once we are in the saddle.

It has often happened to me that a horse feels threatened by the line, rearing and bucking against it whilst I try to lunge him. It requires a bit of time, after which, understanding that it is not a real threat, he will ignore it.

So to summarize, lungeing the horse is helpful to achieving a lateral mise en main (in the hand), with interaction of direct yielding. Moreover, it is useful to begin to move together with the horse, by running next to him in all three gaits to make him understand that we will be with him during the movement, setting down the basis for getting in the saddle in the future.

Let's remember to take into account the attitudes of the horse imparted by natural flexion that greatly influence what we have done and what we will do. A horse who is flexed right will always retain those characteristics, which can only be mitigated after long and efficient corrective gymnastic work. The word 'corrective' can seem brutal, but the right effects really depend on how we tackle the exercises. A good gymnastic programme will be hard, but it should never lose the characteristics of respect, and should be progressive. On the other hand we must tackle problems as they come up – it's all about how, as always.

CHAPTER 19

Surcingles, Saddles and Other Strange Things

When is it time to put something on the back of the horse? When he willingly accepts all the exercises that we have done to date, when he lets us clean him, accepting the repeated contact of the grooming tools. (It is no more natural for him to let us clean him in all the crevices of his body, than it is for him to carry a saddle!) When his trust in us becomes evident on the basis of his responses to the actions we carry out on him. There isn't a precise moment in which to do it, but there are many moments in which not to do it. The important thing is not to do it in these moments.

Trust.

A test of trust in work at liberty is that of circling round the horse, who naturally should remain still.

After a halt, we should approach him, walking towards the withers or the shoulder, gently stroking him first on the neck and then on the haunches, moving so as to circle him without ceasing to touch him. It is important to maintain a physical contact because, at a certain point, whilst we are moving towards the haunches to pass to the other side, he won't be able to see us, but will always feel us and be aware of where we are. If we decide to do this exercise, we don't stay too distant from the horse for fear that he may kick. If we have doubts, we go back to the exercise and carry out a more careful desensitization, with the schooling whip as an extension of our hand. Otherwise, we stay as close as possible to him, firstly to make him feel safe and secondly to be safer ourselves. Let's make a mechanical analysis to understand this better. When the horse kicks, the impact reaches its maximum power when the leg is almost fully extended, therefore by remaining close, we may be thrown away from the horse but will receive a minor impact. Clearly it should not happen and there will be every reason why this does not happen. If you think 'this is not the moment', postpone the exercise, until you are sure that it is. Spend time well.

When we move around him, we don't make sharp movements and always observe his attitudes; if he remains quiet with his head facing forwards, we can proceed. For us it will be difficult to understand his facial expressions, but his ears will always be clearly visible. We speak to him softly to reinforce the contact; if he moves his ears to listen to us, that's good; if he puts them back and whisks his tail with annoyance, it's better to stop; he is not yet happy with our presence there.

Let's go back and start again.

Having gone round once, we repeat the same thing without touching the horse. We will still use a vocal contact, but no physical contact. We should always read the state of the horse before our every movement, ready, should the need arise, to interrupt and re-start from two, even three steps back. We never watch the clock when we are together with our horse. We gauge the passing of time, based on the progress that we make together, without worrying about the length of time, but rather the quality of it.

We will be rewarded by not watching the clock …. An objective assessment, at this point, should indicate to us that we have all the assumptions to be able to proceed. A calm horse, who permits us to move quietly around him, touching him, going around his perimeter, leaving his field of view without getting upset, indicates that he has confidence in us and in what we do. He doesn't check us out in a suspicious way; he will be attentive to our requests, ready to collaborate, yet relaxed. If we have this state, we can safely go ahead and, whatever we do, whatever new thing we introduce, it will be necessary that he finds this tranquillity every time, with every new thing, before going on. It doesn't matter whether it is a small or big change, what matters is that he adapts to that change before facing a new one. If the horse is not yet calm on the lunge, we need to identify the element worrying him and work on it; to saddle him would not advance our work with him, but would simply add another problem on top of an unresolved one, which would always continue to haunt us. We tackle all the problems objectively; we can, and must, resolve each one before increasing the work load. Always bear in mind that 'when we try to bury a problem, it then takes root'.

Necessary Equipment:
- Numnah
- Surcingle (or elastic belt)
- Saddle with elastic girth

The surcingle is five to seven centimetres wide, with an adjustable length. They can be easily found on sale. They are used to secure fleece or towelling rugs that don't normally have buckles, to hold them in place on the horse, since they are only used for short periods.

I would advise using an elastic surcingle or girth, rather than non-elastic ones because the latter tend to create a greater sense of oppression to the horse, replicating the capture by the predator, and it's not uncommon for some individuals to fall to the ground when we tighten them. Even when the horse is more advanced in his work it's wise not to do the final tightening of the girth in his box or in the place where we normally saddle him. It is better to always move the horse after the final tightening prior to mounting, and then tighten it gradually whilst he works. I have often been accused of spoiling the horse, in that he is not still whilst I tighten the girth. But this is not true. I could easily ask the horse to stand still and, if necessary, I do, but in my view, this avoids stumbling onto numerous problems. Mine is not a vice, but a good habit. I have seen many a rider not manage to move their horse one step after mounting, and unceremoniously end up in the dirt. Therefore, the fact that he moves before mounting, ensures that he does afterwards. It's also a good final check to ensure that everything is okay.

The surcingle is the first thing that the horse should accept. I prefer to introduce this on a lunge line. Should it provoke a state of panic, it will be easier to control him, putting him on a large circle. At liberty there is the danger that he might injure himself if he loses too much control in direction or speed, involuntarily bumping into something or trying to perform too abrupt changes of direction, in order to free himself from the surcingle.

Many 'gurus' of equitation claim that when the horse bucks trying to free himself of the surcingle or saddle, he does it because he is not ready and we have not 'respected' his timing.

Nonsense! The horse bucks because he is not born with a saddle and trying to explain this by metaphysical means, is to deny reality, proposing a vision of a horse who is no longer a horse, but a being adapted to our ideas of convenience. The buck is part of the horse's nature. It is a very normal rebellious act that indicates the volition of the horse to feel free, proud of his own nature and way of being, using all his energy to conserve this state. He wants to move freely, without impediment; his survival and his pride are at stake.

When, in nature, I see a horse carrying another horse on his back, I will be happy to accept an alternative version.

That is not to say that the horse will not accept this change of state, indeed, with time, if our relationship with him remains consistent and respectful, he will arrive at a sense of collaboration and togetherness in our work.

But, for the moment, we let him show us his disappointment. He does not have a vision ahead or, if he has, surely at the moment it's not in line with ours. He can't possibly imagine that our intent is, amongst other things, to get on his back. Leave him to run his course. He will soon realize that to buck or bolt serves only to shake off dust and he will eventually realize the futility of such a gesture, always reverting back to the primary need – for conserving energy.

Not all horses buck or bolt; this depends on their subjective capacity to tolerate changes of state. Above all, it does not mean that a horse who is initially more tolerant than another, will be better.

Therefore, we can prepare our horse all we want, but if in the moment we put on the surcingle, he bolts or bucks, we shouldn't be surprised – nor should we be if the opposite happens. The important thing, as I have already said, is not to proceed if we have skeletons in the cupboard. There is a moment when we can do it, and there are many others when we shouldn't do it yet. We ask ourselves then when we shouldn't do it, and the answer will arrive of its own accord.

The Surcingle

We act: the horse is on the lunge line in our left hand and the surcingle in the other hand. Let's always remember to clip the line to the side ring of the headcollar and to change the clip over every time that we change sides, for whatever reason. If he runs off, we will always have the correct pressure on the headcollar.

We place ourselves as always, at the level of the withers at the centre of the school and start to 'play' with the surcingle. We let him sniff it; if he wants to he can bite at it a bit, without overdoing it. After that we bring it near his neck as if it were a brush and we make the gesture of cleaning him. From the neck we pass to the shoulder, back, haunches and so on, on both sides. It will be a good move if we manage to do this also whilst he's moving, putting him in walk and continuing to use the surcingle like a brush, taking care near his sensitive parts and always staying in a safe position.

When the horse accepts all this in a calm and casual manner, it will be the moment to proceed.

We pass the surcingle, or the elastic belt (this is recommended the first few times) around the horse, immediately behind the withers, where the thoracic spine begins. (It should be adjusted so that it will be fairly taut once done up. If it slips and moves backwards towards his stomach it will be a disaster. But we don't overdo it; he's not a lemon and we shouldn't squeeze him – we just ensure that it is well fitted so that it can remain in place without slipping while following the movement of the horse.) We go on to retrieve the surcingle from under the horse, grabbing the long part of it hanging on the opposite (right) side, but gently, first by touching his left shoulder, stroking him, taking our hand downwards until we retrieve it from the other side. But we never stop touching the horse with the hand doing the retrieval.

We always remember to watch the horse's attitudes, through which we can assess his state, always ready to go back and repeat whatever we need to. If the horse runs off while we try to retrieve the two sides of the surcingle, we have made a mistake; we have pushed him too far and have not made the correct assessment. It's not a tragedy, but we must start again from square one. Once we have the two ends of the surcingle, we start to let him feel a bit of pressure, tightening and slackening the elastic without doing it up. Once he has accepted all of this, we keep a constant pressure for a few seconds and then take it way again. We should repeat this a few times before finally doing up the surcingle.

We should then move a few steps back from the horse into the neutral position and prepare ourselves to make him go forwards. It is now time for him to experience all this whilst he moves. We should expect everything and nothing. We ask him to take himself forwards. We calmly ask for the walk, then trot and canter. If he reacts by bucking, immediately make him go forward in a decisive way, in an energetic canter, by using a determined request. If he runs off, let him do so without trying to stop him; when his energy diminishes, he will start to assess whether this is really of benefit. If he doesn't, all's well and we can ask for a few transitions in the gaits and reward him. Before changing direction, we should be sure that he is calm and that he has accepted his new state in all the gaits.

In the following days, his defensive reactions will become less and less and in the end he will accept the work willingly. Never forget to keep him happy with long pauses and lots of stroking. We should familiarize him with the surcingle by moving it towards us, undoing it and doing it up repeatedly, and so on

The Numnah

We should proceed with this in the same way; we start by letting him play with the numnah and then using it like a brush etc.

Once the numnah is in place, we should fix it using the surcingle.

The Saddle

As above – nothing changes, but maybe we should remember, for the first few times, to use a light, uncumbersome saddle, like an English saddle and to remove the stirrups. When the time comes to re-attach the stirrups, we make sure that they are not adjusted too long so that they don't bump against the horse's upper forelegs.

THE BIT

Is it necessary? Yes. For de-contraction. There is no other system. The headcollar on its own will not make the horse de-contract, though interaction between the headcollar and the snaffle bit will, on the other hand, bring about the use of the snaffle itself in an increasingly passive way. (*See* Chapters 21 and 22.)

But it's not yet the moment to discuss this; we will look deeper into this topic further on. I usually put the snaffle bit in immediately after the horse has accepted the surcingle. It takes time for him to get used to the feeling of a strange body in his mouth. When my daughter had braces, it was not easy for the first few days, but after a while she didn't notice them anymore.

On the market one can find a myriad of different and useless bits, many of them even dangerous. This is great for the trader, but bad for our culture. All we need is a simple full-cheek snaffle bit and nothing else. The material can be discussed, but the form should be that. The cheek bars are needed in that they apply an external pressure to an inside request, somewhat like the headcollar.

The first time we put the snaffle bit in the horse's mouth, we need to be very careful. Remember that we are dealing with extremely delicate and sensitive organs, the tongue, palate, bars of the mouth, lips, with millions of nerve endings. The rule will be to be delicate.

We approximately adjust the bridle, holding the straps in such a way as to be easily adjusted, without putting them through the keepers. Some people spread the bit with substances like honey to make it more pleasant; I don't. I do, however, make sure that it is really clean and doesn't have any substances on it that can upset him, like saddle soap or metal polish. It is also essential to be aware of the temperature of the bit. In summer it can be burning hot if left under the sun and in winter it is freezing cold if left outside. It can be held in the hand for a moment to let it reach the right temperature. This is a form of respect for the horse.

I never put the bridle on by standing behind the horse's head and passing my hand from the other side. Instead, I stand to the left of the head and hold up the bridle with my right hand

Punto di Reschio, head collar and bit.

then, with the left hand positioned and open under the bit, I carefully make contact with the horse's lips, taking care not to hit the bit against the closed teeth. At this point I gently insert my index finger into the corner of the lips (where there are no teeth), keeping a contact on the lips with the bit in the palm of my hand. I brush the tongue with my index finger to stimulate swallowing and, when the mouth opens, I gently insert the bit as far as the corner of the lips, taking care that in doing so it does not hit the teeth. After this I do up the bridle, keeping the snaffle at the corner of the lips. If it were to be lower, it would hit the teeth.

The same care should be taken when removing the bridle. We undo it and keep it at the height of the corner of the lips, lowering it gently. If necessary, we stimulate swallowing as described above.

I often see riders rip the bridle from the horse's mouth and pull it down as if it were nothing. There is nothing more dangerous. Always avoid doing this.

We must also put the reins on, and shouldn't take for granted that the horse will accept them, securing them to the saddle so that that they don't impede any movement of the horse. They must be loose and should not yet be used. The aim is that the horse becomes used to the snaffle bit and the reins whilst we carry out our work with the surcingle or saddle on the lunge line.

The correct adjustment of the bit is when it rests firmly in the horse's mouth in the empty space between the incisors and the premolars. We must always be very careful not to let it come into contact with the canines, or tusks, which are present in males from five years of age. (I have also seen females with tusks and we should always inspect the horse's mouth from time to time to check its state.) If we use a leather bridle, we must remember that there can be contraction or expansion of the material, and so the adjustment must be checked periodically. In short, the bit should always be checked before one starts work. It only takes a few moments to ensure that all is okay, and we owe that to the horse, out of respect.

A snaffle that has too thin a diameter can be upsetting to a horse during pressure, whilst one with too thick in diameter can be cumbersome. Correct width is also important – it mustn't rub on the sides of the mouth, nor there be too much play in it.

For the moment it suffices to place the horse in a bit and to continue our work without using it.

CHAPTER 20

Inseparable

We must now get the horse used to our close presence. Our intention will be that of remaining 'stuck to him' during our exercises. He has accepted lots of things up until now, and now he must accept us.

With the horse under saddle or with a surcingle and a bit, we place ourselves at his side and start to stroke him until we are hugging his back immediately behind the withers, making him feel our contact, both with our arm and the side of our body, gently pushing against him.

Normally horses willingly accept this contact and relax. If not, at this point we will know how to proceed. With the horse still, and while still touching him with our hand, we can start to carry out a series of desensitizations, starting to move ourselves on the spot jumping up and down for example, at first very slowly then, as the horse acquires calmness, increasing our efforts with bigger movements and always getting ever-closer to him. We could gently tap the saddle with an open hand, dance, sing, even mime the act of getting on his back. In short, whatever we want to do. We should always proceed rigorously step-by-step and pause every time we note annoyance or intolerance in response to our actions. If the horse runs off, as usual we have overdone it and we should go back to square one. The objective is that he doesn't run off. It all depends on us.

Having done that on both sides, we should ask him to move off in walk, staying close enough to him so that we are touching him with our right hand 'on the left rein', holding the line with our other hand, so that we put him on a large circle with his head lightly flexed in our direction to avoid risks. The danger here is that the horse can escape in our direction (even in response to an involuntary external stimulus – we should always be prepared for everything) and trample us. With his head lightly flexed and on a circle, this eventuality is avoided. He can see us, and the light flexion (which can be reinforced if need be), will stop his haunches from sweeping us away, as he will prefer to move forwards toward the outside. If the flexion were external, the haunches, rotating around the shoulders, would inevitably move towards the inside, where we are standing.

If the horse seems initially unsure of taking himself forwards with us in the correct position, we could use a schooling whip to gently stimulate him (lesson of 'go forward'). We should proceed with the same exercises as done with the horse at standstill, jumping, dancing and so on and always moving closer to him so as to be able to touch him and subsequently, throwing ourselves against him. I repeat, we should proceed step-by-step, stroking him and always rewarding him.

We should never, but never, have an aggressive attitude when we carry out these exercises. The horse knows only too well the difference between a dance done as a sort of game and an aggressive act. We should start with slow movements and gradually increase their intensity.

We should also remember to maintain a position of safety that protects us from any possible defensive actions.

We should start by holding onto the saddle and sharing our weight with him, gradually teaching him to take the weight, adjusting his balance, first in walk, then in trot and finally in canter, at times with a slight jump with our arm around the saddle, hanging onto it on the way down. We then relieve him of the load and thereafter repeat the exercise, always performing it on both reins. A little bit like when learning vaulting.

THE APPROACHES

These are needed to further desensitize the horse, increasing our safety. We need to get on board and the more things he has done, seen and tried, the fewer the surprises for him and for us.

We put the horse in a circle of five/six metres with the lunge line. We should start at walk. From our position, we approach him until we hug his body with our arm over the saddle, continuing the movement and then moving away again and returning to our original position.

The novelty for him is in the movement.

Seeing us approach from a distance, he could easily interpret this as an aggression – therefore we need to be careful with both his and our attitudes.

Because of this, I would strongly advise you to start this exercise the other way around, starting therefore from a position close to the horse, hugging him and putting him in movement, and then moving away and coming close again. This will be more understandable to him, in that we were already together during movement and he has only to understand the two transitory phases: the going away and coming close again, always maintaining the gait. In this case, the first transitory phase (to go away) will be easier for him to accept owing to the expansion of space as opposed to its compression (the coming close).

We should proceed in a progressive manner and be very careful always to maintain the neutral position of safety. Should we, in error, transmit an aggressive message to the horse, he could instinctively take a defensive attitude and we must be protected from it. No one's perfect, neither us nor horses. We will inevitably encounter mistakes on the road to understanding and being understood but, armed with patience and resourcefulness, we will achieve our objective. The road is long and there are many possible dangers, which must remain precisely that – 'possible', not 'actual'.

As the horse's tolerance grows, so should the intensity of the exercises. We should pass on to trot and, if we are physically fit, also on to canter, making our approaches always quicker and more sudden, varying the weight and the length of time, increasing both until we are hanging from the saddle and holding onto the horse while he is moving.

If, whilst we are approaching, the horse tends to stop, it's not a problem. In fact it means that our horse is a thinking horse who prefers caution in the face of uncertainty. It will be easy for us to teach him to maintain the gait, thus giving him security, and the more he feels we are determined, the more he will acquire the necessary awareness.

If, on the other hand, the horse runs off, it means that his defence mechanisms are still too reactive when he works with us and this is not good. He sees us as a threat and is ready to react. We should proceed to desensitize him of it. The problem is that, if he runs off whilst we are executing an approach at trot, we should in theory maintain this state until he understands that there is no danger and therefore flight is futile. This is easy to say but not so easy to do. But there's a remedy for everything and we can proceed as I have said before, with the inverse exercise – starting near the horse and, having gone away, then going near again.

Then, the moment he starts to defend himself by escaping, we should try to stay close to him, holding on tight to the saddle and trying to follow his movements without hampering him. We should immediately try to get a pronounced flexion of his neck and put him on a tighter circle, so that his flight always gets more uncomfortable, until he calms down.

On the other hand, this kind of exercise, 'the approach', has this specific purpose – to assess to what extent the horse will collaborate, defend himself, or is simply trained. We seek his collaboration with ambition and, if our work has been good, sooner or later we will have it – the important thing is not to get discouraged and to have confidence in the technique, especially if we are insecure and have no confidence in ourselves. If we respect ourselves, horses will respect us; if we overestimate ourselves, they will underestimate us. However, if we underestimate them they will not overestimate us, but just ignore us. Someone has to lead, and if we don't, they will. Not through nastiness (in these cases sentiments tend to be dangerous), but simply because decisions have to be taken and the person responsible, to whom one refers, has to be identified.

Mind you, to be responsible for someone is no small thing. Horses, like us, are born with this need for leadership in their DNA, and their part in this hierarchy will depend on experience and surroundings, but they must nevertheless always have their own place.

Can a follower become leader? No! Or rather, he will become one only if events dictate. It will never be his ambition, but rather a constriction. It is not in his nature and he doesn't have the stimuli to take him in that direction.

Of course, there are various levels of follower; there is no fixed scale. A horse could be more or less likely to follow, but I repeat: ambitious horses do not exist, only horses with characteristics that will make them no more or no less than what they are.

Some people are fulfilled by directing, and responsibilities are an integral part of their way of life; others give priority to other things, but what really matters, what makes us feel 'good', is the fact that things are done in a fair and coherent manner, both for those who direct and those who are directed. A very aggressive and incoherent mare will never become head of the herd, simply because she will not be followed and will not be trusted, whilst a strong, decisive and coherent mare will be taken as an example, earning respect day-by-day. Horses will put us to the test and the fact that they share our decisions will be neither gratuitous nor guaranteed. Our state must be demonstrated and maintained. For this reason I often speak of consistency. The attitudes that we have, the actions that we carry out and, more importantly, how we behave, will be continuously assessed by the horse, especially in the initial phases.

Horses are what they are and they assess things as they are. A mirror reflects an image without altering reality. We stand naked before them and to them, who are without false illusions, the results of our actions will always be obvious. Assuming that we are strong enough to actually look in their 'mirror', what we will see will be nothing but the truth, and the hardest truth to accept is without a doubt the one that shows us our mistakes. It will be even harder to change and to go back and retrace our steps in a different way.

All this verbosity to say that we have made it! When the horse accepts all this with ease, the moment has finally come to give him the 'gift' of our weight, in the sense that gravity will no longer be our problem. In short, it's time to get into the saddle; of course the saddle must be on the horse, otherwise it doesn't count.

THE EMERGENCY STOP

In the mounted horse, this consists of making him yield his haunches (disengagement) with an accentuated lateral flexion of the neck. In theory, it is useful in emergencies (rearing, bucking, the horse bolting off, loss of control and so on) to remove the haunches from under the mass of the horse, so that he loses reactive power.

With the help of an accentuated flexion of the neck, which creates a further imbalance, this should, in theory, prevent the horse from making defensive manoeuvres. In theory.... but in practice this is a 'red herring' (with all due respect to herrings, wonderful fish that they are).

First of all, when a horse bucks, stopping him by disengaging his haunches is the last thought that comes into one's mind. This is because, in trying to stop him, the haunches take on even more power under the mass.

Secondly, if the horse bolts, he bolts. And I would be curious to see how one disengages the haunches of a horse in full gallop.

Thirdly, if the horse is in defensive mode, to stop him is never a good thing. Movement is always the key to everything, even and especially in defence.

Fourthly, if you are mounting a stallion, be careful. I have already seen a horse flex his neck and bite the leg of the rider, then throw himself to the ground on one side without letting go with his teeth.

Therefore, if you want to, go ahead and teach the horse the emergency stop. By now you have the knowledge to do it. However, I do not advise it.

Be sure, however, that the lessons in the forward gaits are nice and clear in the horse's mind, because this will be the one real thing that can get you out of trouble. Always. Let's make some hypotheses without analysing their causes. Let's say simply that we have found ourselves, for unknown reasons, right in the middle of a storm of bucks in quick succession. First of all, let's look at how a buck occurs mechanically.

The quarters move suddenly under the mass, producing a vertical push, which is all the more explosive the slower the forward movement. This means that the less push that is used to go forward, the more it can be used to produce a vertical movement. The maximum power that a horse can dispense is more or less always the same. Much depends on how this is used and especially what the conditions are for it to be available during a certain movement. Therefore our defence against a buck, mechanically speaking, can only be to make the horse go suddenly forwards. The more we make him go forwards, the more the arc of the buck will be widened. The wider the arc, the easier it will be for us to stay in the saddle, being subjected to less violent vertical movements. This mechanically, but also from an educational point of view, will produce nothing other than an accentuated and inefficient effort (uncomfortable condition) that the horse will tend to avoid in the future.

The problem is that, for us, this is not instinctive. What we would like to do is to grab on and to pull with all our might to interrupt that movement, but this would just accentuate it. We should by now have come to terms with our instinct and be able to master it. Our well-being depends on it.

The same is true for rearing, or the horse who tries to bite us.

The only exception is for the horse who bolts, in which case the only response is to try to bring him into a controlled circle (assuming we have the space for it) trying to calm him down, but without making too many requests. It's always better to wait for the result of physical exertion to take effect, as this produces a natural change of state. As soon as he starts to understand that there is nothing to flee from, and flight does not produce the required effect, things will change radically. In contrast, trying to hold a frightened horse, especially a young subject, does nothing but increase the tension, accumulating the energy already produced. It is always better to let the tension find a controlled outlet. More importantly, we need to keep in mind that, in the initial phases, we have an approximate control, and that even the horse can't yet manage to control his emotions. But we can control one thing; the direction. Even if the receptive conditions are almost non-existent on the horse's part, the unilateral request (to put the horse on a circle though an internal request) will still be efficient. Bilateral requests, on the other hand, cancel themselves out (strong requests on both reins that make an induced leaning). Therefore, the best thing to do is to stay calm and maintain control of direction.

Let's not think too hard of ways to stop our horse, but rather of sending him forwards, always. What's more, if we need a handbrake, we have probably made a mistake in our means of transport. We can certainly find the appropriate dealer, and nowadays the accessories are infinite: ABS, heated seats, rain sensors … but the last time I tried to install air conditioning, the horse did not like it very much and actually, even the mechanic was a little surprised.

SUMMARY

Let's take a look at everything we have done up to now.

In work at liberty, we have introduced ourselves to the horse, we have made him understand who we are and what our respective roles are.

Then, working together, through use of the body language, we have carried out some exercises:

- The 'go away'
- Control of the gaits
- Change of direction
- Halt
- Pushing and drawing-in pressures
- Rotation of the shoulder around the haunches
- Rotation of the haunches around the shoulder
- Backing-up
- Going forwards
- Sensitization
- Desensitization
- Flexion of the neck, laterally and vertically
- Voice association
- Direct pressures

Then we have carried out other exercises to increase his tolerance, using the surcingle, the saddle, the bit and then ourselves. Finally we 'offered' him our weight, so that he could adapt his balance to this change of state.

All of this in a coherent manner, listening before asking, and learning to read his expressions and his state.

What we've achieved is no small task and, at this point, I am sure that our language has already taken a more dialectical and confidential form and that both our and the horse's levels of understanding and mutual tolerance have come to that point where we don't give 'orders', but 'invitations' and where the association is becoming a mutual sense of partnership.

Naomi Statuti with Dorado.

And it is precisely at this point that we normally dissipate all the riches accumulated up until now; when we climb into the saddle.

Everything that we have worked so hard to learn is forgotten. Our hands don't manage to communicate, to establish a contact; we no longer manage to make ourselves understood. Our body doesn't manage to adapt itself to the forces unleashed by the movements of the horse. We feel lost, in an alien world, on an alien's back. We are not only a weight – no, much worse – we have become an unstable load, unable to communicate and practising an equitation consisting of negatives (or absolute demands). Our requests become abrupt, with very few and inefficient yieldings. We don't manage to help the horse – we just hamper him.

In work from the ground, as soon as we came across a problem, somehow we managed to overcome it. From the saddle, this does not happen, and even a small problem manages to create a crisis, by becoming an insurmountable obstacle which, in turn, triggers off others.

Our vision is distorted, our observation point changes and with it also our attitude. Our involvement is much more direct and part of the horse himself and this involves a loss of identity, resulting in indecisive and confused actions. Our role as leader is lost. As the saying goes, 'in work from the ground we speak, but in the saddle we 'babble'.'

We are no longer autonomous in our movements; instead, we depend on the horse and this loss of physical independence creates some emotional problems for us. From the ground we tend to have control; in the saddle we tend to lose it. There is the possibility that it won't be us who decides where to go; it's no longer our legs that support us; and it's no longer our mind that necessarily takes the decision of what we do next. We need to share, and the art of knowing how to make the horse carry out our wishes is necessary.

The fear that our mistake might have direct and immediate consequences for us, with possible physical repercussions, is real.

Two bodies of a different nature – ours and the horse's – unite and, in that union, one of them assumes the burden of carrying the other. Two minds of a different nature must remain divided so that one can lead.

If we lose our identity, we will lose the ability to decide. At the same time, sharing is required; our body must assimilate the horse's movement and his mind must assimilate our intention. Only thus can we be as one with the horse, maintaining our essence without trying to change his.

In the union between a man and woman, moments of really great sharing can be reached, but as much as we may lose ourselves in one another, our identities and our roles remain distinct. What I am trying to say is that it is not necessary to be identical to feel united; in fact it's really when we want to make someone the same as us that we can gauge how distant they are from us. All this requires understanding and if we think about it, everything that we have discussed up to now, is nothing more than a treatise on precisely that. Now we need a stable contact. Compromises are useless. Our hands have a serious but, at the same time, beautiful job to do. This cannot be carried out if they are not dissociated from the forces that the movement of the horse exerts on our body.

The horse's movement in the three gaits needs to be dealt with in different ways.

- At walk we must follow the natural movement, with our hands following the movements of the head.
- At trot, instead, in order to maintain contact, our hands must be still in spite of the increasing forces that our body has to deal with, in that the horse's head, in trot, does not move or oscillate.
- At canter the horse's head is not still. Seen from the side, it makes a light elliptical movement that extends downwards and forwards, and then returns upwards and backwards, with different timings. i.e. short when it extends downwards and forward and longer when it rises and goes backwards. To make the concept clearer, taking into account the three

Tatiana Milne Skillman on Casanova.

beats of the canter, we note that the head's highest and furthest backwards point occurs in the suspension before the first beat of canter, that is, between the end of the third and the beginning of the first. The ellipse then progressively accelerates into a downward and forward movement until the third beat when the cycle is then repeated. Naturally the hands must make the same movement if we want to maintain contact, in an elliptical anticlockwise movement from high to low following the above-mentioned timing if we want to maintain contact. Clearly, timing will tend to vary in respect of a fast extended canter or a collected canter.

It is natural for the horse to move in this way. For us it is not. We must learn this and learn it well, very well.

The main problems in communication have always been rooted in the inability to follow these movements effectively.

Do not underestimate this aspect and be sure to disassociate the movement of the hands from the forces exerted by the movement of the horse. Until then, remember that it is better to have no contact (very long reins) than an approximate contact. The horse's mouth is very delicate and it is our responsibility.

NOTES ON RIDING WITH SEAT AIDS

This topic, naturally, should be developed according to the discipline practised. However, for now, since this subject risks becoming too time-consuming, I would like to try to offer a simple synopsis that can be safely implemented.

Many of my students ask me: '… but can the horse be driven by seat aids?' The answer is that the horse must be driven with them. The problems and misunderstandings that arise when talking about this topic stem from the fact that it is not taken sufficiently into account that the seat aids are a language – the most refined one. To be able to express and then to be understood, when we communicate through our seat aids, we need to master them. If we are

The seat aid is a powerful instrument and requires care.

in difficulty in following the horse in his gaits, clinging with our hands to keep us in the saddle, how can we try to express ourselves through our seat aids?

The seat aid is a powerful instrument and requires care. At first, it is necessary to learn to manage it through its neutrality. It's a bit like the neutral position in the body language working from the ground. The seat aid's neutrality must be evident in all the gaits; and it will result, in practice, by following the horse, making sure that both our weight and movement are appropriately responsive for that particular movement, for that particular horse, in that particular exercise. Once we are able to do this following without disturbing, we can start to interact with our seat aids. The rules are the same as we have used up until now so, as we have included the vocal language in the work from the ground, in the same reference to syntax, we will include the seat aid's language in work in the saddle. Through variations of our balance and therefore of our position, we can produce associated requests. For example, to ask for a halt we should proceed as follows:

- Sit with our shoulders behind the vertical, weighting the back of the saddle.
- Move legs back without touching the horse.
- Increase pressure on the reins until the horse indicates signs of stopping. Then repeat.

In a short time, it won't even be necessary to pass to the phase of pressure on the reins. The horse will understand if he is educated to do it.

This is a simplistic example, of course, on how the seat aids can become an effective means of communication. However, we should always consider which is the correct seat aid for that exercise, on that horse, in that moment ….As you can see, the more we go forwards, the more the variables increase; variables that in this point of the book will be really too many. Then, what should we do? Simply, we should see the seat aids for what they are and try to master them through a neutral phase. A neutral seat aid is not a passive one. A neutral seat aid is able to follow the horse's needs without interacting or interfering with him. This is, in fact, not easy or obvious, but a nice goal to reach that will lay the foundations for future interactions. Don't believe those who try to teach the 'correct' seat aid to activate the correct muscles of the horse … no, it doesn't work like that. The seat aids are a language that must always be consistent and therefore have to be adapted to that particular exercise, for that horse, in that moment. Are you tired of hearing this phrase yet? Good – I'm managing to convince you through exhaustion!

Another very important thing to consider if we use a seat aid as a communication factor, is that we should understand that the horse perceives it as a variation of balance and weight. Now, the perception of these variants, for the horse, will be all the greater the more that he finds himself in an unstable equilibrium. A well-collected horse will be more able to feel even the minimal change of position of the rider; this ability to react to the seat aids will be less evident in a horse in extension.

Above I have introduced a topic that we have not yet discussed; that of stable and unstable balance, which we will discuss further on.

For the moment, let's consider the seat aid as no more than it really is.

We have to be dynamic by adapting ourselves to the movement of the horse (and not hindering him) by keeping a neutral seat aid. All this is easier said than done. However, it should become natural and instinctive; the horse should become an extension of ourselves whilst each one of us maintains their own individual characteristics. We have to feel and to feel good with him, creating the appropriate conditions in which he can feel and feel good with us.

CHAPTER 21

Interaction between the Headcollar and the Bit: Introduction

I often asked myself, during the first phases of training, whether there was a method of alleviating the annoyance that an interaction, however well performed, causes inside the horse's mouth.

Everything that I saw around me failed to convince me. The bitless bridles have a closing action that does not help de-contraction without which, as far as I am concerned, equitation doesn't exist. The various 'ethological' bridles of different types with more or less contraptions didn't work for me either. Not to mention all the nosebands or closures that can be applied with more or less padding – they really are coercive. Yes, yes I know, it all depends on the hands that use them, but regardless of all that (one can see horses who bear the signs of similar instruments and will do so all their lives) I didn't like the idea of having to use coercive instruments to the detriment of communication. All the things mentioned above (and many others) are coercive instruments. (It is strange how the human mind puts its efforts into inventing things that cause pain instead of trying to find the correct path to a solution.)

I wanted to find something different, which based itself on communication pure and simple, always present, without compromise. If communication were to be ineffective, the

Maria Francesca Patrizi on Punto di Reschio: extended trot.

level of cooperation or the mental and physical preparation inadequate, then all this had to be apparent rather than masked by instruments of coercion. The horse should carry himself and we should, to the best of our ability, help him and prepare him to do so. This was the idea, radical and pure.

But I found nothing. I looked everywhere and I must admit that, at times, I came under the illusion of having found something, but it remained an illusion for a long time.

I come from a family who, for many generations, have cultivated the art of making do and so one day whilst I was working with a young horse I made a mistake and clipped the reins to the rings of the headcollar (I had left it underneath the bridle for convenience) instead of the snaffle and it suddenly occurred to me that there was nothing to invent; I already had all the equipment, I just had to use it.

If I was really convinced (and I was), that a wall of air was sufficient to interact with a horse, a headcollar used for grazing should suffice.

So decided and enthusiastic, head down, like a bull charging an obstacle, I started to work with just the headcollar. But I soon had to raise my head again and dampen my enthusiasm because the results were disappointing. The horse leaned heavily, especially in gymnastic exercises, and all my attempts to persuade him did not suffice. At times he would respond, but much as I struggled to communicate with him, paying attention to every tiny change of state, this rarely brought perceptible results and I only managed to achieve the appearance of lightness without actually being able to achieve basic gymnastics. I did not manage to communicate in an efficient way. I was disappointed and heartbroken but I didn't want to surrender. I thought I had cracked it but, in the end, I had to admit that the reality was different. Precisely that, the brutal and harsh reality, reality…

…Just a second, isn't a horse perfectly able of reacting to an association if educated to do so?! One could just create an association … but with what? Wait, wait … the snaffle bit, isn't it able to de-contract him with the swallowing effect? What if he managed to associate the two things? Perhaps it was still do-able … perhaps ….

Yes, that is, more or less, how the idea was born and, just as in every birth, joy always follows pain. It wasn't all joy and flowers, especially at first there were some huge disappointments. But what I can now affirm is that, often with surprising results, the method works and has been tested on many horses, youngsters as well subjects being re-educated. I can easily affirm that many individuals who came from a

Silvia Montanucci on Silber Falke, bitless. Sooner or later she'll stop denying the obvious.

'traditional' working background appreciated it and learned in a better way. I believe that I have often had the sensation of reading a sense of gratitude in their eyes, or maybe that's what I wanted to see. Or maybe not. The real reason why I am trying to diffuse this method is not for glory, but out of the conviction that it efficiently helps the communicative growth of the rider, while reducing the annoyance, the intolerance and the suffering of the horse, even when he is in inexperienced hands. It is far better to have inexperienced hands on a simple headcollar than on a bit. It is not a compromise, but an alternative method based exclusively on communication and psycho-physical, hence motorial, knowledge of the different types and of the morphological conformations of horses. Certainly, it is not easy to understand and carry out, but it does have a peculiar characteristic … it is honest, transparent, and therefore not masked by constraint or force. Lightness is thus not only obvious, but necessary, so that it can be implemented.

A horse who carries himself with the simple assistance of a headcollar, is nothing more than the natural result of an education based on effective collaboration. It could not be otherwise.

The bit contributes to maintaining the responses of the horse on the headcollar 'fresh' and lively and the headcollar does the same for the bit.

This is because, especially in the initial phases, we will not make requests on only one or the other instrument, but the frequently changing variations of the request keep the horse much more vigilant compared to requests made on only one instrument. This variation brings many benefits in terms of the horse's attention.

An element that allows changes to the degree of comfort of the request, such as a request on the headcollar, can induce a considerable incentive to rational collaboration.

Surely, its usefulness consists in allowing the horse to make the choice of lightness and collaboration; choice that he will be able to make at our every individual request. He will always have the option to decide not to cooperate or to oppose; in which case the punishment will be de-contraction through the bit, which is not coercive but nonetheless uncomfortable. Alternatively, he will simply choose to comply with our requests, which will remain light and coherent on the headcollar. This will be the real incentive to cooperate. It is and always will be, however, his choice and you can be sure that he will make that choice. Never doubt the sensible decision-making ability of your horse, but rather ask yourself if you are capable of putting him in a position to make that choice. In other words, if we make the right requests, he will, in time, give us the right responses.

With time, the use of the bit will assume an increasingly passive form and the rider will therefore be able to decide whether to use it or not, but whatever the final choice, the rider will have arrived at it through the use of a technique that tends to develop reciprocal understanding, and with the utmost safety of the horse and respect for him in mind.

The time it takes? It is certainly not slower than other methods and, what's more, we develop the correct awareness of the moment in which the horse starts to use self-carriage in the various exercises, and this helps us to understand the correct progression of work while completely respecting the horse.

It does not offer a short-cut or quick fixes, but embraces the continuing search for the horse's collaboration and his athletic training.

HOW DOES IT WORK?

The quick and precise response through non-coercive associations must necessarily be a choice that the horse makes each time. We cannot just expect it but we have to obtain it; we

Maria Francesca Patrizi on Punto di Reschio: passage.

cannot oblige him, we have to convince him. As they say: 'the road to hell is paved with good intentions ', but this is not enough for us. We will rely increasingly on facts, never on ifs and buts. First of all it requires conviction; certainty will follow with experience.

We must work on the contact and never on the leaning, which the horse may offer us or which we may induce in him as an easy solution. Always remember that the horse will find it easier to create rigidity, to exert strong pressures or oppositions on the headcollar. It is not a coercive instrument and should be treated with extreme3delicacy, never using force. If we abuse it, we will immediately pay the consequences. Don't worry, this isn't a death sentence. If we err we can always recover, indeed, since it is in no way traumatic, we will rarely have defensive reactions from the horse, only reactions of comfort. In any case we should not allow these as they induce passivity to the aids, which is potentially damaging. This last fact was the problem that occurred most often when I initially used the headcollar alone. Therefore, the association with the snaffle is required, since the headcollar on its own is not capable of effecting de-contractions efficiently. For example, let's say that we wanted to ask for a yielding. Let's assume that our horse holds his head too high, with the tip of his nose too far out and we, through a bilateral pressure of the headcollar, carry out our request. If the horse, choosing comfort, opposes us, then we have no other method of dissuading him from doing this. We cannot communicate with our body, since the language of attitudes is not practicable in the saddle.

Especially during gymnastic and stretching exercises, where we often put our horse in difficult and challenging postures, he will surely look for a way out of them, and if tolerating a strong pressure on the headcollar were to prove more comfortable than yielding to the request, we can be sure that this is the path he will choose. Therefore it's not that he doesn't feel the pressure of the headcollar – indeed he is perfectly aware of it – it's just that, by his nature, he will always choose the situation which is more comfortable for him (conservation of energy). We need an additional instrument when the horse tends to make these choices, and the snaffle has the right characteristics to be able to do this. In fact, if it's used well, when the horse makes an opposition to the headcollar, without taking the pressure off (we mustn't interrupt the request), we should also make a request to de-contract using the snaffle, thus obtaining a yielding which the horse will associate with the request of the headcollar. All this works very well and, with time, the action of the snaffle bit will become more and more passive, up to the moment when it is no longer necessary. It is not Utopia, and the responses of the horse will always go hand-in hand with his athletic training and ability to do the exercises. Clearly, if we ask of him exercises that he is not yet capable of executing, we will have the same negative results whether we use the headcollar, the snaffle or devilry of some sort.

In the end it will be our choice whether to take the snaffle bit away or not – we can easily leave it there in a passive manner. At times, just knowing it's there is more important for us than for the horse, and should the need arise ….

To clarify this a bit, the requests that are made on the headcollar must never be interpreted by the horse in a passive way, but in an extremely ready and reactive way. Often, when riders who don't know and don't practise this method ride my horses ask how to use the four reins, I always respond, 'Use them as you wish, it's not a problem.' This is because, in terms of both reaction and contact, my horses don't differentiate between the bit and headcollar and often they don't realize where the request was made.

Of course, this is the result with horses who are already advanced in their work. With a horse who is just starting, clearly it would be different. This is the goal to be pursued, in that it is achievable.

It is very natural for horse to react to associations, especially if the associated request provokes less discomfort than the primary one.

It will become a choice of ease.

FIRST STEPS

When we are dealing with a young horse and the exercises are relatively simple, such as when taking the first steps under the saddle, I always use the inverse canon. I create associations with the request of the snaffle bit through the headcollar. Thus horses learn to accept the use of the snaffle bit much less traumatically and more progressively.

This is because, initially, the horse is usually left to his own balance until he learns to move more freely in the three gaits balancing our weight, even if he tends to assume incorrect postures that are potentially dangerous to his structure. In the initial phases, expecting to make him assume the correct position for that particular exercise could create too burdensome a workload.

Therefore:

1. Request on the headcollar (primary)
2. Pressure on the snaffle bit (associated)

This should continue until the horse freely accepts simple requests with the snaffle, that is without the rider applying the pressures that provoke reactions of annoyance or opposition. We should not seek a stable contact extended over time, not yet, and our requests will just be indicative.

Be careful – simple requests must be just that – they should only be used to direct the horse where we want to go, for example on a large circle. They must not, under any circumstances, be extended and continuous requests. Remember to return immediately to the headcollar each time that excessive difficulties are noted.

The time necessary for all this can vary, but this is not important. During this time the horse will develop his capacity to change his own balance, adapting himself to carrying our weight in the three gaits with exercises that we will use to influence changes to his position, even if they are wrong. For the moment, the position assumed to execute every exercise will remain his choice. The fundamental thing is that he always takes himself forwards willingly.

While we limit ourselves to indicate the direction and the gait, we should nonetheless commit ourselves to reading the horse's attitudinal reactions; how he feels on a large circle on the right rein in contrast to the left rein, at trot rather than canter, and so on. He doesn't have any secrets to hide; it's up to us to know how to read him properly. We must understand his difficulties and his strong points, the positions that he assumes that could be right and therefore strengthening, or wrong and therefore potentially dangerous. To understand his way of doing things will help us to educate or re-educate him, and gives us a real sense of belonging and partnership that goes beyond absolute demands, enhancing adaptability in mutual partnership. Our horse is always telling us about himself, we should listen to him before we act.

For example, we could note the natural flexion in a young horse and the attitudes he assumes on a circle or a straight line. How he takes himself forwards, whether he raises his neck up too much to lighten up his shoulders, or alternatively if he tends to keep it too low….

Every attitude that the horse assumes will be his 'natural' attitude; this in no way means that it is correct, but neither is it necessarily damaging. It depends; some attitudes should be corrected as soon as possible, whilst others could prove to be real strengths, solid hinges, on which to build remedies for our uncertainties and, believe me, we will need them. It is right at this point that, with a level playing field, we could have an 'easy' or 'complex' horse.

The more his natural attitudes are 'correct' (naturally in line with the execution of the exercises), the fewer the re-educative exercises. This means that if, for example, owing to certain physical conditions of build, or by attitude, a horse tends to reverse his neck-line, the time that we need to dedicate to corrective gymnastics will not be comparable to that needed for an individual with correct attitudes. We must also remember that, in an individual with serious morphological and reactive defects, these very 'defects' will always be ready to reappear, even after an intense period of gymnastic re-education, in that they are part of the natural way of being of that horse. He is like that because he 'is made like that' and these are his natural attitudes. This does not mean that we should surrender ourselves to them, especially when they are dangerous. We will always try to improve and help our horse, but at times nature is obstinate.

A rider spends his whole life trying to straighten his horse, rarely does he succeed.

OLIVEIRA

We will see that to understand the problems or strengths of our horse will not be so difficult after all. We can always count on one thing; his honesty.

Remember, 'He is what he appears' and this is one of the very few cases where appearance doesn't lie.

We just need to know how to look and if, in order to do that, we had the eyes of a child, what we would see would be nothing but the truth.

To see what we want to see is too easy and damages the horse.

STABLE CONTACT AND DE-CONTRACTION

At this point, the horse will know how to move quite easily in simple exercises carrying our weight. Now we need a more articulated form of communication and for that, we need a stable contact which, in turn, requires a stable balance (on our part), which has to follow the horse in every phase of work. The action of our hands cannot follow our need to balance; our legs are not anchors and neither is our back ….

Taking for granted that the necessary prerequisites are acquired, we proceed, reminding ourselves that at this stage it is best to use the rising trot, adjusting the diagonal according to requirements. We will consider this matter further on.

The horse willingly accepts the 'contact' provided that this is what it is. Having already dealt with this matter abundantly, I will say no more.

A request differs from contact in that it exerts a pressure, which can be more or less intense but never excessive. The normal consequence of pressure is either a yielding or (when it has caused an annoyance) an opposition. De-contraction is the correct cure. To facilitate the correct reaction (de-contraction) one must limit the annoyance that the pressure of the snaffle bit transmits to the palate and the tongue, which in some cases can provoke the defence of withdrawing the tongue from the pressure, causing it to retract into the inside of the mouth, and to force the contraction of the jaw bone with opposition to the bars, or of going over the snaffle (tongue above).

Various ways of holding the reins.

Method that I use.

A simple and efficient solution that avoids all these problems is to execute a 'high request', so that the snaffle bit doesn't exert pressure on the tongue but on the inside of the lips. By going up inside the mouth, the snaffle also stimulates swallowing which, in turn, activates the de-contraction.

Of course, this high request, introduced by Philippe Karl, should not be made regardless of circumstances; we do not need to have our hands high all the time we ride the horse (as one often sees). It should be carried out only when needed and then interrupted immediately after de-contraction.

We shall start therefore with a 'classic' pressure and wait for the horse's reaction. The moment in which de-contraction occurs, we should be ready to cease our pressure. All's well.

If, instead, we incur opposition, without releasing pressure (I repeat, without interrupting the pressure), we take our hand (or both depending on whether it is a bilateral or unilateral request), higher, so that the snaffle rises to the inside of the mouth, lightening the pressure on the tongue and stimulating swallowing. Once de-contraction is obtained, we should follow with our yielding of the hand, which should go gently towards the horse's mouth, returning to its normal position. By repeating this in the correct way, our horse soon will associate this with the classical request for de-contraction, thus eliminating his opposing reactions. To make a high request directly, without the normal one first, will become counterproductive over time.

The procedure is as follows:

- Normal request or 'classical request'
- Assessment of horse's reaction and, if needed:
- High request
- De-contraction
- Normal position
- Repeat until we obtain the correct reaction to a 'normal' request

The high request is, as far as the bit is concerned, a great cure, but like all medicine should only be taken in case of need. Therefore, we by all means use it every time we deem it necessary, but we don't make this (as often happens) our only mode of guiding or communicating with the horse.

Once we have established contact in the horse's natural position, and once that contact is stable, this will be the moment to start interacting in a deeper and more constant way with him. Up until now, we have not tried to change his position and consequently his balance and way of tackling these exercises, but perhaps the time has now come to apply a different concept.

POSITION

The position is nothing other than the shape the horse assumes for a certain movement. Every movement has a correct shape, therefore the more correct the shape, the better the exercise will be performed.

A ball rolls because it has a spherical shape. If it had a cubic shape, to make it roll would be somewhat complex and our only other alternative, in order to obtain the same result, would be to modify its shape, naturally within possible limits. We are not in the bargain basement of the obvious, but often the simplest things escape us and the position is of fundamental importance, just as is its correct interpretation. Let's not make the mistake of looking for positions that are too artificial, as one often sees in competitions, just to obtain a higher score, because that's what the judges want. Our only judge is the horse and we must refer only to him. So evaluate very carefully his motorial requirement and the position that is best adapted to help him develop with gymnastic and appropriate exercises.

We are tied to precise physical laws and, were we to understand them, we could make them our allies instead of opposing them, even when it is unnecessary to do so.

All this is to say that the horse, much like us, can be 'moulded' in what he does. Or, if we prefer, he can be best prepared. A piaffe has a shape, a passage has another, just as the half-pass, or shoulder-in … and the more correct the horse's shape, the better the possibilities of performing a correct exercise.

Now we must understand another concept. I have just said that a piaffe, for example has an ideal shape. Perfect.

In fact, this ideal shape varies according to the type of horse, to his difficulties or strengths, which are tied to his natural attitudes. Not only this, but this shape also varies with the progression of work. With a young horse, I often tend to do exercises that concern 'collection', with a certain degree of 'extension' of the neck, in order not to load the hind legs to the detriment of their movement. This is not nonsense – indeed, the earlier we learn the concept that there are no academic positions to suit all horses, but rather variable positions adaptable to the horse and not vice versa, the better. Therefore, we must understand that the position must vary (if we really want to help the horse) based on various factors, all perfectly connected and discernible from time to time.

The neck-line of the horse plays a very important role in all of this. It has the power to displace the weight from the shoulders to the haunches and vice versa, modifying the axis of the spinal column and much more. It therefore follows that managing its position is fundamentally important to us. Obviously, to interpret this in a correct manner we need a lot of experience, but there are lifelines, positions that are almost always correct in certain moments of work, for almost all horses, which we can use even though we don't have an extensive understanding. Obviously, it could not be the ideal position for that particular horse, but it will certainly never be a damaging position and that's no small thing.

This shape, this position is the following:

- Head that tends towards the vertical (never beyond).
- Neck-line extended along the horizontal of the back vertebrae, or slightly higher.

Is that it? Yes, that's it.

This, in the initial phases or in re-education, brings numerous benefits. But be careful, with certain types of horses, it's easier said than done.

For example, horses with a long back and a neck-line that tends to be inverted (strong underneath): this position stops the vertebrae of the back from rounding, reinforcing the abdominals and stopping the hind legs from activating themselves without receiving excessive loading. The horse's back is very important and we must take this into careful consideration. Obviously, a horse with a long and heavy neck-line it is not ideal, since this will increase the weight on the shoulders, but an extended position will nonetheless allow the hind legs to be dynamic, reinforcing the abdominals and, unless we hold the position for too long a time, it will rarely be damaging.

In any case, according to where we want to move the weight, one thing is certain; we must learn to manage the position of the neck, depending on the muscles involved, without coercive instruments, preparing the horse for self-carriage.

Irene Boriosi on Tigris: extended position, head on the vertical with the projection of the neck on the horizontal of the spine.

EXTENDED POSITION

Interaction between Headcollar and Bit

Trying to move the position of the scales is a good exercise in communication and in correct positioning. Of course; because either we are able to communicate, or we use force to obtain what we want. Let us assess our ability.

Firstly, the tendency to … (this is the most important part of the book): let's get it out of our heads that the horse will do exactly what we have in mind when we make a request – this will not happen. Clearly, this refers to educating a horse and not to a horse who has already been educated.

The root of education lies in capturing the intention to execute. We must show the horse the correct path and follow it with him. Let's assume that, for more or less correct motives, we want to position the horse's forehead on the vertical when it is above it. We must not imagine that we can do so with pressure, that is, pull it towards the vertical and take away the pressure only when the position is correct. In fact, this will never happen, instead we will probably unleash reactions of opposition (especially with low requests on the bit) and consequently we will apply coercive instruments such as gags, draw reins, changes of bits and so on (happy suppliers!). No, we must think and act in a different manner. Let's imagine that, in order to achieve our objective, we must go up or down some steps. Now, let's imagine that we are not in front of these steps, but our horse is. He doesn't see any objective, he sees only steps. We cannot make the horse understand our objective inasmuch as he doesn't see it and he doesn't see it because he doesn't need to. For him, it simply doesn't exist. If we want to make

Roberta Bocchini on Sereno: another example of extended position.

any headway, we will have to see things his way. Remember 1+ 1+ 1 +1 … it is the moment to apply this concept.

Situation: horse in front of steps (let's imagine them wide, adapted to him). What will the next request be?

All those who answered, 'go up the steps', were wrong. The request should be 'go ahead' walk, move forward, movement. When the horse has moved himself, what should we do? Continue to ask until we have reached the top, inasmuch as we have given him the direction and we now incite him to continue.

Correct? Wrong! We will have to interrupt the request and start again. If necessary, even step-by-step. We mustn't reward the 'fact' that the horse goes up, but his intention to go up. To interrupt the pressure means okay, we are on the right path, continue, we are doing well, we are almost there. So we incite him to do and to do again and above all, we establish the principle of collaboration, implementing the concept of the comfort zone. In the sense that we make the situation comfortable we 'take the pressure away' the second the horse shows his intention of doing.

The timing (*see* Chapter 7, Timing) is of fundamental importance.

Therefore, in our case of the forehead on the vertical, we will need to achieve this in steps and to interrupt the pressure every time the horse tends to bring himself on the vertical, and keep a constant pressure when he seeks a different route than this. This is logical from the horse's point of view. Of course, the positions should be maintained on the basis of the preparation of the horse, with progressive work.

To better understand this topic, it is perhaps best to clarify some of the terms which, though specific, can often create some confusion.

- On the vertical (when the horse's forehead is perpendicular to the ground at an angle of 90 degrees).
- Above the vertical (when the horse's forehead is forward of the vertical, forming an angle greater than 90 degrees with the ground).
- Behind the vertical (when the horse's head moves back toward his chest, forming an acute angle with the ground of less than 90 degrees).

These positions do not, however, indicate the conditions in which the horse is 'on the bit', which are:

- On the bit (ideal condition in which the horse searches for contact keeping the reins stably and lightly stretched, ready to follow the rider's hand by varying the positions of the point of equilibrium).
- Above the bit (the horse tends to escape upwards with decisive and heavy opposition to the bit.
- Evading the bit (the horse evades contact, moving his head towards his chest).

I would like to point out that this terminology, even though it is appropriate, always highlights defects in the horse but does not explain that these problems are induced by the rider. Having said this, I would like to bring the reader's attention back to the fact that there is often a degree of confusion with these concepts. For example, a horse 'behind the vertical' does not necessarily always mean one who 'evades the bit'. In fact, in certain conformations of horses, certain stretching exercises may require the horse to be behind the vertical while still being on the bit.

Pirouette.

I will never tire of saying that to manage positions is different from inducing oppositions. Remember that this last concept is always valid. For everything.

Let's come back to the request: forehead on the vertical, example of positive response:

- Request of yielding on the headcollar.
- Yielding of the horse.
- Yielding of the rider, who follows the horse's mouth, maintaining a 'LIGHT' contact. (Don't fall into the trap of false requests with a contact that is too heavy), until getting to the desired point.
- Stop the hand when the horse finds himself in the correct position.

This is the ideal condition, which initially rarely happens though, or better, could happen; it's just that we normally find it difficult to maintain that position. Muscle memory is missing. What is muscle memory? Many scientists all over the world are working to find concrete answers to this question. We know that it exists, we know how to activate it, we just don't yet know how it works.

I have found a very interesting article, referring to dance which, in my opinion, is the discipline that is closest to the gymnastic exercises that we perform with our horses. Dancing, as opposed to other disciplines, contains a large percentage of HARMONY. Twyla Tharp, one of the greatest living choreographers, calls this ability 'muscle memory', the memory of muscles.

It's one of the forms of memory with the most value …. It's the concept on the basis of which diligent practice and thanks to the repetition of certain physical movements, our body remembers those movements for years, even tens of years, after we have stopped doing them.

Whilst Wikipedia says:

[It is] is a form of procedural memory that involves consolidating a specific motor task into memory through repetition. When a movement is repeated over time, a long- term muscle memory is created for that task, eventually allowing it to be performed without conscious effort. This process decreases the need for attention and creates maximum efficiency within the motor and memory systems. Examples of muscle memory are found in many everyday activities that become automatic and improve with practice, such as riding a bicycle, typing on a keyboard, playing a melody or phrase on a musical instrument …

Therefore we can understand how difficult it can be for a horse, to maintain certain positions when they are unnatural and constricting and how absurd it is to seek such positions through the use of anti-educational instruments that oblige the horse to develop musculatures of defensive opposition. Above all, it threatens the trust and collaboration of the horse, knocking down his mental initiative, reducing him to a machine.

We don't want all that; we want a live, reactive, conscious horse who collaborates because he is educated. And then, we want to be educators, with all that entails, for good or bad, in the sense that we will err, but will always seek to correct by using expressions of the language, never by coercion. We must have the certainty that, if the language is correct, the horse will carry out the request. He may not manage to maintain the exercise, for this we need practice, but he must show the intention of wanting to do it, and if we prepare him well on a gymnastic level, he will execute and maintain it in self-carriage.

Therefore let's take a look at what really happens when we seek to get the position under discussion. We will have varying difficulties in keeping positions that are not naturally assumed by the horse, depending on his conformation. These difficulties will, however, diminish through repeated requests and repeated confirmations through comfort zones, so as to bring the horse, through pressures, to the continuous search of such a zone or position, which will become stable with time (muscular memory).

The procedure is as follows:

- Request with the headcollar, with intervention of the snaffle bit if necessary.
- De-contraction.
- Contact with confirmation of the position (comfort zone through non-request).
- Repetition every time that the horse seeks different routes (more comfortable).

Always remember that the snaffle should be used and should always intervene in case of opposition on the headcollar. It should be used well, every time that it is needed. If we use it like that, we will use it less and less. If the contact on the headcollar becomes excessive, that's not good; we de-contract the horse with the snaffle. If we feel an opposition of comfort on the headcollar, we don't tolerate it too much; we pass to the snaffle bit, and maintain the request of the headcollar. The latter is the really difficult thing to carry out. It requires a fair mastery of the double reins, without which it will be complicated to obtain the correct association. The horse follows very specific thought patterns in learning. If he does not do something, it isn't because he did not understand, but because we have not explained it well. The use of the headcollar and snaffle bit, as I said, requires good practice in the use of the four reins, but it is not always necessary to do it while on the horse. I advise you to always carry some bits of rope or reins with you and manipulate them when you can, simulating the interaction with the horse, especially in maintaining the request on the headcollar during the intervention of the snaffle bit, easing them together on de-contraction and then maintaining a contact on the headcollar. This is the greatest obstacle that stands between us and our horse; the ability to use our hands like we use our voice. It's true, it's difficult, but it's nothing that we can't resolve with practice. The benefits that it brings will be handsomely rewarded.

We should bring our horse to lightness through gymnastics and prepare his structure so that it leads to self-carriage. Lightness is always honest.

CHAPTER 22

Interaction between the Headcollar and the Bit: an In-Depth Look

As we have just said about the interaction between headcollar and bit: Just one element that changes the level of comfort of a request, like the request being outside of the mouth, can increase the horse's attention and his incentive to collaborate in a rational way.

The right responses. This is where the biggest misunderstandings normally arise. Just as with great disappointments, they induce us to change path because of lack of results. It is, however, never the horse's failure to make a sensible choice as much as our incapacity to communicate in a correct and efficient manner. Therefore, the use of this double instrument (the headcollar and bit) is necessary so that the horse can choose effective cooperation. It is, after all, quite simple: the bit alone can never offer the same comfort as the request on the headcollar, which operates outside the mouth; vice versa, the headcollar alone would

Maria Francesca Patrizi on Punto di Reschio: passage.

not offer the possibility of an efficient de-contraction, which is indispensable. Yes, I know, in theory this is all quite understandable, but in practice?

Well, at this point, you will need to carry out a simple exercise that will help you understand many things about yourself. Doing this is very important and very simple and, what is more, it will not take up much of your time.

Take a rein and ask someone (preferably someone with some equestrian knowledge) to help you by holding one end of it, simulating the horse's mouth. You hold the other end, establish contact, and then apply pressure (request), even a strong or intense one so as to put the rein in tension. When this tension becomes stable, simulating a momentary opposition, and the hand of the person simulating the horse's mouth remains rigid and immobile, ask the person to yield without warning, that is to say without your being aware of it, as 'Okay, sometime within the space of ten seconds suddenly let go without telling me.' The horse, himself, doesn't let you know when he is going to yield – or rather he does, but you must be able to read it (which is not easy without the required experience).

At this point we are going to examine what happens to your hand with this sudden yield. If, at the moment of the yielding, your hand does not move backwards or your fingers close, but rather you respond to the yielding by relaxing your fingers and moving the hand lightly in the direction of the mouth, it means that your communication is excellent and that you are perfectly able to communicate your intentions. Bravo! Sincere compliments. In time the horse will seek contact with your hand since he will gain benefit (state of comfort).

The use of the head collar and the bit is necessary so that the horse can choose effective cooperation.

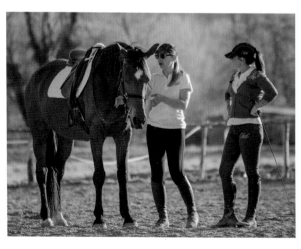

If, on the other hand, as I believe will happen, your hand makes a sharp movement backwards and contracts, even slightly, we aren't there. You are severely punishing your horse at the very moment of his intention to yield and comply with your request. At the next request he will be highly unlikely to choose that path which has produced no benefit. The result? A contracted jaw. A contraction that will extend to all other parts of the horse. His mind is concentrated on trying not to receive pain or discomfort from your hand. He defends himself.

Be careful and don't cheat. Your yielding has to occur at the same time as his. If you yield even slightly later than he does and move forwards a fraction later, it will not work. That fraction, for the horse, is an eternity in terms of the meaning of that action.

All of this, of course, must be seasoned with the right amount of contact, which should not be absent either before (where it all begins) or after the yielding:

- Contact (where everything begins)
- Request
- Yield (horse)
- Yield of the hand (simultaneity)
- Contact (where it all ends)

In any case, at first, don't worry if, in attempting to yield, you lose contact. That's fine. It is far better to lose contact than to maintain a stable but heavy one. This is one of those instances where excessive stability is damaging as it will oppose any attempt at (or rather search for) lightness ... and as everyone knows, to rediscover something you first have to lose it .....

On the numerous occasions on which I have asked people to do this test, very few have achieved acceptable results on their first attempts and, by very few, I mean VERY FEW, perhaps one out of a hundred. But then, in a short lapse of time, practising without the horse, almost everyone succeeded in achieving a discreet amount of simultaneity, such, at least, as to induce the horse to understand the situation and therefore seek out the hand. Don't be disheartened if, at first, the task seems impossible; I guarantee that, with practice, it will seem less difficult. Not easy, but do-able. How many times should we carry out this exercise with the horse? Always! Communication is always active. At the beginning it may be coarse but, with time, it will become more refined until it becomes imperceptible, sweet: remember communication in the herd? Although the shape of the communication may change according to circumstances, the basic foundations will always remain the same whenever you relate to horses, whether in the saddle or on the ground. The more we proceed with coherent communication, the less we will encounter opposition, all the while increasing the horse's sense of co-operation, surrounding him with communicative signals of belonging, which, in other words, are part of his nature and of his *modus operandi* ... thus of himself. He will be at ease with us and will show it.

In conclusion, this exercise should not only be done, but be done often. Hence the more we master it, the better.

Everything we do with the horse is important, but achieving the correct timing of the

Half pass.

yield is, absolutely, the thing to which we should dedicate all our attention and effort, even at the risk of losing control of other situations.

For example control of direction: at this stage it doesn't matter – just ensure that the horse is moving forward and concentrate on the timing of the yield. Up to now, even if I have not always succeeded, I have tried not to be pedantic, but in this exercise one has to be. Even more so if we think that this exercise is carried out with double reins, with double points of contact, one on the bit and one on the headcollar.

The 'correct timing of the yield', in particular our timing, should soon lead us to recognize the horse's intention to 'do'. When we are able to work on this, that is to say to recognize and reward positive intentions, hindering negative ones, we will make another big step in the sphere of communication, perhaps, or rather undoubtedly, the biggest one. Grasping the horse's intention to 'do' is no more than the correct choice of timing through the correct reading of the horse. This produces an enormous incentive in the horse's will to comply with our requests – a horse who cooperates.

These last few lines encompass the meaning of the whole book; they are its key, its cornerstone. If we are unable to understand and implement this, it will be useless to proceed, since it will result in nothing other than an intense sense of frustration, which will not be good for anyone, especially for our horses who are always on the front line when it comes to suffering our shortcomings.

This should not undermine our will, but lead us to carry out the above- mentioned exercises with even greater assiduity. This will help us, with immense gratitude on the part of the horse.

ELEMENTARY METHOD OF FEELING THE HORSE 'ON THE BIT'

So, what is it? I have sincerely been asking myself this for years. There couldn't be anything more badly named, or more likely to induce an incorrect interpretation on the part of the reader. Elementary method of feeling the horse on the bit … what a mystery.

In reality, it is one of the most complex things, especially for the average rider to execute. 'But how so, if it's elementary?'

I have always interpreted the word 'elementary' as an indispensable element, without which it is impossible to communicate. Do you know what this element is in our context? I hope so … it is contact. The whole book is about this. Just think of it – an entire book that talks about the elementary method of feeling the horse on the bit. If you'd have known that, you'd definitely not have bought it. In fact, an alternative title could have been: *Elementary Method of Feeling the Horse on the Bit and its Mysteries*.

Another question that I have always asked myself is 'Who knows what the advanced method of feeling the horse on the bit would be?' It would surely be an incredibly complex thing, which only the very few could achieve.

I'll give you a heads-up, the 'elementary method of feeling the horse on the bit' does not exist, and neither does the 'advanced one', nor does 'leg-yielding'. They're just a beautiful collection of useless words whose only aim is to mislead those who hear them, in that those who pronounce them have no idea of what they are saying. Feeling the horse on the bit, or even better, contact, is never either elementary or complex, it can only be correct.

All the rest; horses who lean heavily in the hand, or evade it, are not being on the bit.

It is something else, but not that. The outcome of correctly feeling the horse's mouth on the bit offers the possibility for applying and expressing a correct language, which will result in lightness. Full stop.

The Double Contact

As if one weren't enough? Who knows what they will invent next? In reality, as we have already seen, loads of things have been invented. Countless instruments of torture that lead the horse to obey and stay on the right path. The only problem is that they don't work and have an unpleasant collateral effect of stultifying the rider. Contact is a complex idea for a rider to digest. Double contact is even more complicated and should not be attempted until one has mastered the timing of the horse's de-contraction on the bit with the horse being stable and light on the bit.

Double contact is complex and should not be attempted until you have mastered the horse's timing.

It doesn't matter whether the horse is capable or not of executing certain exercises, or at what level of training he is. You can teach or re-educate your own or any other horse at whatever stage they are currently in. Remember that you are doing something undoubtedly less coercive and based on the language that will be accepted more than happily by your horse. Therefore he is ready, and has always been ready and open to a constructive dialogue. The real problem is whether or not we are ready. Ready or not, let's proceed, always reminding ourselves, however, that a thing done badly will of course lead to a chain of events that will tend to worsen the situation, increasing the level of misunderstanding, unless it is corrected. Sometimes it is essential to retrace ones steps with a critical spirit.

Let's analyse the double contact; we introduced it earlier, so now let's take a good look at it.

We should frequently repeat the exercise previously described of request and yield done without the horse. This time though, using the double reins, holding them correctly. Our fingers must start to feel the double contact and start to play with it. Passing from one rein to the other, then using both, seeking to make a request first on one and then on the other. The more we manage to do, the more we make our movements supple, the better it will be. Holding the double reins should become a norm for us. Above all, we should become conscious of what we are doing, always trying to understand where our contact or request are prevalent, whether too much on the headcollar or too much on the bit, and so on. Learning to recognize, understand and manage the pressures is fundamental, always feeling on which finger they occur – the finger of the headcollar or the finger of the bit.

If the horse attempted a decisive defensive reaction either on the headcollar or on the bit, this would radically change our consequent action.

An opposition on the headcollar requires a de-contraction on the bit, whilst an opposition on the bit could require a sudden change of the request itself, bringing it higher, so as to make the bit go up inside the mouth, lightening pressure on the bars and stimulating swallowing, de-contracting and then resuming the contact on the headcollar.

Therefore we need the ability to correctly interpret what we do, what we feel and what we see. I don't wish to be a hypocrite in telling you that this will be easy. It will be complex, particularly until we manage to understand the correct associations. From that moment the work will take on an unexpected fluidity, with enormous gratitude on the part of the horse. It is a sacrifice, but if we love him that much, we should be willing to do it. The one sure thing is that we will be rewarded … not in the next life … but in this. I hope.

We continue with the difficult problem of the double reins. The double contact will not always be necessary, indeed, with the passing of time, as the horse learns to associate and understand the requests on the headcollar, the use of the bit will drop suddenly, rendering it less indispensable and, at that point, we can deliberately render it superfluous. But for gymnastics and for educating, it is needed and will be needed for quite a time. Clearly the amount of time will depend on the level of training which we wish to reach. If we should decide to stop at a dignified work on two tracks, rather than execute consecutive flying changes … that is clear and understandable. What is often not so clear is the concept that the horse will be able to maintain lightness and the correct response on the headcollar, only when he is able to do so. So obvious! Well, maybe it is, but it's not a foregone conclusion, especially if our training background comes from a school that often uses heavy mouthpieces or other coercive means. Bearing in mind whether the horse is more or less ready to execute and maintain certain exercises over time, positions, gaits and so on sometimes does not come into our sphere of comprehension or, in any case, is not given the importance that it deserves. The concept that the horse should carry himself on his own and therefore not be supported or obliged to do so is as difficult as that of contact. But to do this, numerous gymnastic sessions are required, which often tend to bore the horse. In this case, insisting on using only the headcollar, without

Extended trot: the great Punto di Reschio.

the stimulus of the de-contraction of the bit, might cause an excessive heaviness on the aids. Once the gymnastic sessions are at a good level – in other words, when the correct level of athletic preparation is achieved, we will know that the horse is physically capable of executing what we require and we will know that the horse can respond to our requests with lightness.

At this point the doing, or rather our concentration on making the horse do, can be directed to the willingness and reactive availability of the horse, educating him in the lightness of the aids. Without such awareness, any educative decision will become complicated, which could make us the instigators of completely wrong achievements. We can complain all we want about the horse's limitations, but if the problem does not lie in their will, but rather in whether they have been 'put in a position to', then our attempt to stimulate, whatever that may be, would not bring fruit. In any case, the world is full of depressed horses and frustrated riders. Indeed, maybe it would be better to say 'frustrated' horses and depressed riders.

- When a horse isn't ready, we can prepare him.
- When a horse is misunderstood, if we can't manage or do not want to prepare him, we will have to coerce him.
- But do not despair, if you decide to adopt this system you will not be able to coerce, but only render him able to do it.

The headcollar requires an efficient preparation, both on a communicative and functional level. You cannot cheat. The horse must effectively carry himself. And take note – it will not be work that requires a long learning process on the horse's part, with infinite preparation, in the sense that he will never be ready – indeed, quite the contrary. As usual, the problem does not lie with the horse. I don't want to say that the horse will be perfect – he has his own problems; everything hinges on whether we tend to resolve or complicate them, and as a consequence, complicate both our and his existence.

THE MECHANICS OF THE ACTION

Once a bilateral contact, both on the headcollar and on the bit is established, we can proceed in two distinct methods, depending on the requirement and the type of reply we get from the horse. He, in effect, will guide our hands through our correct evaluation of his reactions.

Let's therefore return to the concept of the kind of work for that specific horse in that specific moment. If, for example, the horse's reaction were to be in line with our requests (that is, without contractions), we should continue our action on the headcollar and, if necessary, on the bit, without changing our vertical hand position. If, on the contrary, we were to sense contraction, without losing contact and without changing the axis of the wrist, we should bring our hands upward.

What is interesting to note is that as this action has a ' mechanical' effect; it will result in a gradual change in pressure that will pass from the headcollar to the bit (acting on the bars of the mouth), and once de-contraction has occurred, through the descent of the hand, the pressure comes back to the headcollar. With a simple gesture, that of moving the hand first upwards and then downwards, (descent of the aids), we can carry out actions which would otherwise become very more complex. If we keep the right contact, with the correct pressure, the process of the horse's assimilation of association between headcollar and bit will become natural, so that the use of the bit and the action of de-contraction will very quickly become less and less necessary. Obviously, everything always has to be considered in light of the difficulty of the exercise and the point of training of the horse. Our aim is to educate the horse in self-carriage just through communication and the correct gymnastic exercises. We should not seek positions or exercises that are too complicated or inappropriate for that type of horse in that particular moment of his training … otherwise we will get more or less the same results and negative reactions that we would using a more 'classical' method. The only

With this action, a gradual change in pressure will pass from the head collar to the bit.

variant (and it is a most important one) is that, with this system, we cannot coerce. Therefore, if we want the horse to do it, we must put him in the correct condition to do so. Equitation is a set of synergies that are intended to produce harmony. This will become clearer when we discuss collection, which is the natural consequence of previous good work. Many things are at stake when we try to educate or re-educate a horse, both on his emotive level and in terms of his mechanical movement. There are many factors, many variants, many concepts that are simple on their own but, when put together, become complex.

A non-constrictive mechanism, able to take charge of some of the complex communicative issues in the beginning, can only help a rider in the comprehension and in the practice of this work, thereby easing the task of the teacher – especially in the difficult moments encountered on the journey, when the load seems too heavy to bear. This should not be considered as a teaching short-cut, but rather a good alternative, enabling the rider to put the horse in the position to make sensible choices.

The mouthpiece is annoying. This is true irrespective of the technique. (Obviously, we are not talking about annoyance when we see constrictive and violent systems, but of real torture. 'A learned hand can use a severe mouthpiece'… a learned hand shouldn't need to use one and should lead by example!

'It is not important what you use, but how you use it'… it is important! Of course it's important, especially for the horse who doesn't need it!

And now a bit of elementary physics.

In the diagram we can easily see how, by moving the points B and D upwards and downwards, we can have a variable action on the hubs A and C: where B and D represent the rider's hands and A and C represent the bit and the headcollar.

In fact, without changing the length of the reins, we can have a more or less balanced action either in favour of the headcollar, or of the bit, depending on the vertical position with which we apply pressure. This procedure requires a simple action on the rider's part, which will 'autonomously' carry out complex communication. With time, and with the increase of sensitivity, the rider will acquire the necessary fluidity for a finer communication by using only the movement of the wrist and fingers, without obvious vertical actions. This is always

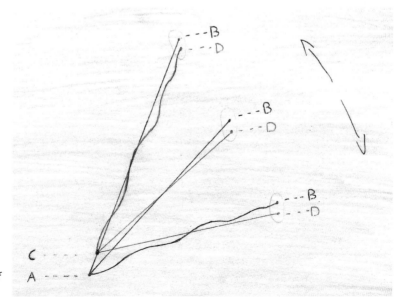

Here, we give the horse the possibility of choice.

provided that the rider receives de-contracted responses from the horse every time: if not, the vertical action of the hand should be used in a timely manner on the bars of the horse's mouth to obtain the correct de-contraction.

That's why it works and why this method can be within the reach of many people. The mechanics of the movement create the correct association.

In practising this, be very careful when bringing the hands upwards; never to lose the contact of the initial request. If that happens, the action is not efficient in that you put the horse in a comfortable position, but in a situation of contraction (involuntary descent of aids with loss of pressure and contact).

The loss of contact during the descent of aids would be less problematical (although not correct) once de-contraction has occurred.

Therefore, if, in the moment of the request, you have a contracted response of three hundred grams of weight (hypothetically) in the action of bringing the hand or hands upwards, you will have to try to maintain this same pressure of three hundred grams until de-contraction, with a following descent of aids. Mechanics will do the rest and, in the movement of the hand(s) going upwards or downwards, the transition between the reins will become automatic and gradual, switching from a singular call on the headcollar, to a bilateral one on the headcollar and bit, then to the bit. Then, with the descent of aids, returning from being on the bit, to the bilateral, and finally to the headcollar. Thus, ascent with constant pressure until de-contraction and descent with contact.

Always be ready to yield the aids at any moment. With time the horse will learn by association and the act of bringing the hand upwards will be sufficient for de-contraction. There will be no need to apply pressure on the bit and soon you will have de-contraction on the headcollar. Always grasp the horse's intention of doing and recompense him promptly. Don't close your fingers and don't change the tilt of your wrist in the upward action, since the mechanical action of transition might be distorted. It is absolutely necessary to hold the reins crossed (the rein to the bit on top) so that the technique is efficient. The precise way the reins are held can be subjective (more or less separation by your fingers of the reins …), but the crossing of the reins absolutely not. The initial contact with the 'low' hand position should become more and more refined with time, until it becomes effective with just a movement of the wrist and fingers. This means that a slightly more prevalent contact on the headcollar is advisable. This discussion was indispensable at this point of the book. This method will be the more efficient the more we are capable of identifying the real problems, their cause, and consequently applying the correct remedy. Even when we understand that the cause sits with us, we must be consistent, we must not be discouraged and should apply the correct remedy to ourselves, with the same attention as if we were applying it to the horse. Every time we consider ourselves equal in rights we also do so in our requests, and the understanding between two beings who have followed a different evolutionary path, but with a common root, will perhaps grow. Before continuing with the technical part, we must deal with another bit of trivia.

NOT ALL HORSES ARE THE SAME

Of all the banalities, this is surely and absolutely the greatest of them all. Of course. And it is even the most complicated. The variables it contains are almost endless. How can you in any way think of educating a horse, both physically and mentally, without knowing him?

In terms of the composition of the language itself, our understanding could take some time, and this is somewhat understandable, but with both horses and us being social animals, with a little practice, we can achieve satisfactory results (especially from the ground; in the saddle, things change). But from the point of view of the muscular and skeletal construction – this is not so. We must understand how his motorial system works. In this case we have very little in common. The simple fact that we are bipeds and not quadrupeds says a lot. It will not be essential to know what the muscles of the horse are called (even though knowing at least the main muscles wouldn't go amiss), or to know the names of the bones of the body, but to understand his muscle and bone structure and therefore his natural balance will be funda-mental. I will try to treat a complicated topic in a simple way, but that's not to say I will succeed. This matter is damn complicated. The physical variables are endless and, for every variable, a whole book could be written.

Let's start by saying that the horse, as a prey animal, uses his speed as his primary defence mechanism. This factor means that the main burden of his weight is naturally on his shoulders. But not all horses have this absolute design feature in static form. Indeed, there are horses naturally built 'more' on the hindquarters. We also need to understand that the horse is not built solely for flight; certainly this is his main characteristic, but thank goodness not his only one.

The real need to make sudden changes in direction without going in a straight line (for example demi-pirouette) is a movement contrary to speed, pure and simple and, to be able to execute this, the haunches have to part-load themselves with the weight that is naturally burdening the shoulders, notably varying both the relation between thrust and engagement and the centre of gravity. All of this is included in the sphere of possible life-saving reactions and is therefore part of normality.

Summarizing this concept, we can say that a horse naturally tends to have a stable equi-

Sara La Grassa on Festosa (student instructor FEEL course).

librium placed at his shoulders, the main characteristic of which is that of moving his mass forward with a predominant ratio of thrust over engagement, or better, with a mass disposed towards a forward thrust. In order to clarify this concept further, let's take as a reference point his centre of gravity, which will tend to move forward in a manner directly proportional to the increase in speed. Consequently, always speaking of a moving horse (not a horse who is standing still or is inactive) a decrease in speed will result in the centre of gravity moving backwards (unstable equilibrium).

This does not mean that this ratio cannot be varied according to need, but – and this is the important concept to understand – the variation of the ratio leads to a large expenditure of energy, and the more the horse is designed and naturally built to produce speed efficiently

Piaffer on the shoulders: note how the weight is intentionally shifted onto the shoulders and the supporting front legs come to the aid under the mass. In this way, the hindquarters gain confidence in the movement. Having to bear less weight they gain in activity (someone might say 'absolutely incorrect').

(propulsive horizontal thrust and centre of gravity forward), the more the engagement or support will be uncomfortable and inconvenient (propulsive vertical thrust and centre of gravity backward).

These concepts could, however, be misleading as they are incomplete.

When we refer to thrust and engagement a degree of confusion often arises. I would like to approach this topic in a different way.

Engagement is the capacity of the horse to bring his hind legs under the mass, but this capacity sometimes tends to limit activity.

One must be very mindful of these things. The addition of a third element helped me considerably in understanding concepts that are apparently simple but difficult to digest. This element is the capacity to carry weight.

This differs from engagement inasmuch as engagement is the action of bringing the hind leg under the mass. The same hind leg then prepares itself to carry weight and subsequently produce thrust.

Engagement produces the movement that prepares the hind leg for support and which is followed by support itself. The phase of engagement and that of support are two completely distinct phases.

The greater the capacity to support, the deeper the action of engagement will be. The greater the capacity to support the mass, to carry weight, the more the movement will be active.

Naturally, all this is, to a great extent, linked to the unstable equilibrium that we will discuss later, especially in phases of collection, but it is important to understand that, if we request an engagement when the horse still does not have the capacity to support weight, this will cancel out (or reduce) activity and therefore thrust. Unless, of course, this engagement is intended to produce a horizontal thrust for extended movements. In this last case, mass is, in fact, moved forward and the point of equilibrium in the movement is stabilized towards the shoulders (to be precise, in horizontal thrust we should imagine this point placed ahead of the shoulders so that they move forward).

Furthermore, if, in the attempt to produce vertical thrust, weight proved to be excessive, one hind leg would be unable to support it and would require the assistance of the other hind leg, thereby increasing the support base and cancelling out activity. Why?

If we analyse the hind legs in their alternate movement (trot), we will see that engagement, once produced, cannot be modified and the distribution of weight can only be varied by varying the point of equilibrium or the rate of speed (variation of the centre of gravity). Thrust can be dynamically modified, but engagement cannot. To be clearer, once the horse has placed his hind hoof on the ground, this position can no longer be changed as it is the base of support, and what happens following this is the direct consequence of this action.

Obviously, in nature, a horse is perfectly aware of his capacity to handle weight, of the movements he intends to make, and is therefore able to adapt engagement to intention.

In equitation, however, things are complicated both by the physical weight of the rider and by that of the rider's often absurd requests. Since engagement cannot be changed once it occurs, if a horse is not adequately prepared, he will defend himself by engaging less the next time around and producing less thrust, or varying the weight by increasing forward movement (varying mass by the movement in his centre of gravity), or by changing the position of his neck (varying mass by position), or rather intervening with the other hind leg, trying to divide the load and breaking the gait.

In the case of generous but unprepared horses, which is the worst thing of all, their integrity and health will be affected by the occurrence of increasingly larger physical problems.

…advancing in the training we should bring the weight to the haunches, which will be ready to support the mass without losing activity (note how the front legs move further away from the mass with greater engagement of the rear legs). Managing the weight and therefore the balance of the horse will allow us to always help him in the progression of work, whatever it may be ('absolutely correct'). Dogma often hinder advancement.

Excessive requests for collection in cases of unprepared subjects will often produce an increase of engagement to the detriment of movement. Our constant request to maintain activity will lead the horse to an instinctive reaction in the improper use of the point of equilibrium, raising his head, hollowing his back, lengthening the base of the trapezius muscle in an attempt to unload his hind legs, with a resulting drastic drop of thrust. In this way the lumbosacral spine will suffer the consequences.

Every time the musculature of the horse is unprepared, he tends to make up for this by changing position by contracting and, where this position is incorrect, his skeletal structure will suffer.

Only through the control of the positions, by rendering the horse's actions smooth and dynamic, can we help him to move in a way appropriate to that particular moment and exercise. This control must be executed prudently. Today, we often see horses constrained to do a piaffe in absurd positions. In competition, it has become normal – almost the standard – to see horses execute piaffe with hyperflexion of the neck . This is certainly not helping the horse through control of the position, but rather the complete opposite of the principle. And what we see in competition is only the end result; try to imagine for a moment what it is like at home, what procedure has been used to produce such a result ….

Engagement and the capacity to bear weight while maintaining activity (thrust) can be seen as one thing; moreover they must become one thing. In the learning phase, however, the distinction between the two will help us understand certain reactions of the horse, helping us to break down even his asymmetry.

Hence, engagement is the act of bringing the posterior of the horse under the mass, but the capacity to bear weight is a successive phase to engagement, albeit a consequential one.

It is absolutely not guaranteed that, if a horse can bring his haunches under the mass, he can then support it. In young horses especially, such an experience could become a strong disincentive.

I would like to bring to your attention an interesting question, to which I have dedicated a lot of time and which I intend to deal with at length in a second book, when we will embark on working on two tracks.

We have all heard *ad nauseam* that the asymmetry of the horse results in a functional diversification of the hind legs, that is: 'one that engages more than it thrusts and the other that thrusts more than it engages'.

Having ascertained this, I have always asked myself whether, in an effort to balance engagement and thrust, the horse found it harder to balance one or the other.

That is to say, in his attempt to achieve this balance, does the horse find it harder to increase engagement in the leg which naturally engages less, or the thrust in the leg which naturally thrusts less?

And if the horse has to work harder to thrust (clearly I mean vertical thrust in a collected horse where the hind legs bear a heavier load), could it be because the leg that has to receive such a thrust is not then ready to support it?

Or could it be that he engages less because the thrust produced by the other leg is insufficient to produce an adequate engagement?

Continuing with our structural analysis, we will encounter horses who are flexed right, left, on the haunches, on the shoulders, those who have necks that are short, long, heavy, light, attached high, low, medium, that are strong above, below, with long backs, short backs … and what about the inclination of the shoulders or of the legs, the head, the mouth … asymmetry … the weight of the rider, which varies with each discipline and, effectively, riding position.

Too many variables. The beauty of it all is that you can mix and remix them as many times as you want and the result will always be different.

Now, the problem of whether or not Mother Nature has dealt us a low blow in her effort to achieve perfection could very well be of no interest to us at all, in the sense that diversity is beautiful, peace on earth, and so on ….

The problem is that, in all this diversity, we always strive for the same goal: a horse who is collected, light and has other desirable qualities. This is to say that, from initially diverse forms, we want to achieve one ideal and common final one. Our ideal, our idea of perfection.

On this point, we and Mother Nature do not share the same points of view. She tends towards flight and we tend towards unstable balance. Thus we are obliged to modify, manipulate, interact …. What a pain, couldn't we have had a pre-packaged standard product to work with? Obviously not. Or rather, we try with artificial selection but, in spite of all our efforts, some groups of rebellious genes continue to escape our control. Taking for granted that we cannot deal with every single diversity, I can only suggest that you treat each specific case by dividing the horse into four principal parts so as to form four well-defined zones, which could be, for example: head and neck, shoulders, trunk, haunches. Having done this, consider each single zone separately, individually, as if it were separated from the others, in order to understand each different element, subsequently reconnecting them as required. Not clear? Let's take a crude example, let's take a horse built 'downhill' towards the shoulders (that is, with the haunches higher that the withers). Without further information on this particular horse, we know that the weight is heavier on the shoulders (heavier as opposed to a differently built horse). Since our objective is to have an 'even' redistribution of weight between the shoulders and the haunches, which will vary from time to time and according to the type of work, we should know that:

A horse at a standstill, not moving, with a 'natural position' has 1/9th of his weight on his shoulders.

If mounted, one has to add two-thirds of the weight of the rider (this ratio will also vary according to the attitude of the rider, sitting and so on). If a rider weighed 60kg, 40 kg would

Matilde Radicchi on Davinci di Reschio.

be on the horse's shoulders. This only serves to give a very general idea, a point of reference but nothing more. Yes, because this is where the famous variables come into play. Coming back to our example of a 'downhill ' horse we will note that the ratio of weight on the shoulders will not be 1/9th but noticeably larger. How much larger? That depends, for example on the neck-line. Long, attached low, with a massive head are all things that increase the weight on the shoulders.

Now let's take into consideration just the neck of the horse and imagine that it is long and strong underneath, that is to say with very developed muscles on the lower part of the neck, with a high attachment.

The best gymnastics to try to develop the correct muscles in the upper part of the neck, lightening and de-contracting the lower part, will be to arch the neck with the head at the vertical. We will see later how and to what degree we will achieve all this, but for the moment let's take it for granted that we can manipulate the positions as we like.

Therefore, the more we round this arch, maintaining the head at the vertical, the better. The lower neck muscles will tend to de-contract while the upper neck muscles will be extended, part of the weight will now shift back towards the haunches and we are all as pleased as Punch. Provided, of course, that the horse keeps his hind legs dynamic, that the back handles the weight received from the shoulders and the rider, and that the horse is well formed – in short that everything is in the right place and all the reactions are correct ….. Can you hear that alarm clock ringing again?

In reality, things are often not like this. We could be faced with a long and weak back that doesn't allow the hind legs to support a larger percentage of the mass. In this case, the optimal position of the neck would damage the back. Therefore, we would require gymnastics and an optimal position for the back as well, which, in this case, would be an extension of the neck on the horizontal line of the spine. In practice, precisely the opposite of what is required to balance out the shoulders, as they would suffer the increased weight produced by the shifting forward of the neck. The neck muscles, as well, would find little benefit in this without the arch.

So what to do? On which factors should we base our choices?

Referring back, we recall that the head and neck, shoulders, trunk and haunches are the fundamental parts.

The head and neck in particular are the most mobile parts since the major sensory organs of the horse are located in the head and need to be constantly and quickly redirected.

Depending on the type of horse, we need to establish the priorities. We carefully evaluate what type of horse we are dealing with: just as we have evaluated the character, so now we must evaluate the structure. We analyse everything both while he standing still and moving freely, always remembering the basic principles and trying to apply them to the various requirements.

The first of these principles is that equitation is dynamic. The solution to every problem lies in movement. Don't try to resolve issues in a static manner; this is never a good solution.

Hence the horse must move forward. Whatever we do that undermines this is never a good thing. Before going any further, the horse must be moving forward.

Secondly, the head-carriage tending towards the vertical is another good thing. (Possibly slightly above the vertical, especially when dealing with young horses.)

The neck, as I have said, is very mobile and has a great ability to shift weight between the shoulders and the haunches and vice versa. However, before excessively redistributing the weight to our liking through the neck, we should, in movement, try to achieve and maintain rounded shapes. Anything that is concave does not make for good equitation. To make a horse round in movement, independently of the particular physical structure of the horse, is normally one of the first objectives to achieve.

Initially, we should always try to shorten the horse's outline by de-contracting the lower lines and extending and mobilizing the upper ones, while relaxing the lateral ones.

When I begin work with a youngster or need to re-educate a horse, the first thing I am careful to safeguard is his back. The dorso-lumbrosacral muscles connect the vertebrae at the base of the neck to the pelvis. The extension of these muscles is fundamental, since their contraction or stiffening results in the back assuming a concave, passive shape rather than a convex, active one. The only system with which we can have an extension of these muscles is through the extension of the neck-line towards the horizontal. This situation will, in fact, put the horse onto his shoulders, but this works to begin with as it will not be a permanent condition and, in any case, will bring more benefits than not. The haunches, for example, carrying less weight, will be more dynamic, active and ready to push the horse forwards. In any case this is a gymnastic and stretching phase which prepares for collection, although 'to prepare' is not 'to do', but rather 'to predispose'. Moreover, an extended neck-line with the head tending towards the vertical also tends to bring the shoulders forward through the brachiocephalic muscles. Flexing a neck that tends to stretch itself will always be easier than trying to do it with a short and contracted neck. The gaits become wider and deep in that the centre of gravity moves forward, promoting the willingness of the movement, the very root of equitation. I cannot claim to know the construction of your horse, but I am almost certain that if you try to extend the neck-line, the benefits that it will bring will be notable. We must not be afraid to move the centre of gravity forwards, putting the horse, as it is vulgarly said, onto his shoulders. This is a desired and sought-after situation, which will help us to prepare the horse for collection. If anything, in the moment of collection, the obstacle will be to have a contracted horse who is struggling to maintain impulsion.

Clearly, you could find yourself confronted with a problem of morphological construction, or moments of training that require different things but, in any case, reverting to request an extension of the neck-line should never be absent, whatever type of horse we meet or whatever type of training we are doing. This will always accompany you, even and especially when doing more advanced work, like a warm-up phase or relaxation after a session of collection – or indeed, any time that it is deemed necessary. I still do this and will continue have this requirement independently of the level of preparation of the horse (although clearly varying the timing).

Therefore, before we delve into situations that are highly complicated, like the specific analysis of typology and correct application of the various gymnastic exercises, we should teach our horse to extend his neck-line.

EXTENSION OF THE NECK-LINE

Working on the intentions of the horse will be our priority. If the concept of feeling the horse on the bit is clear and its application efficient, bringing the horse to extend his neck-line will just be a normal consequence of previous work well done. If our horse seeks our hand because it is a comfortable situation for him, merely moving the hand forward will induce him to seek it maintaining the contact with our varying position.

Should this is not be the case; we then have to take a moment to review how to proceed. We always keep our principles in mind and try to remain consistent. From walk, initially with long reins, we apply a light pressure, asking the horse to go forwards into rising trot. If we get a correct response, then we absolutely avoid asking continuously that the horse moves forward; we do not repeatedly stimulate him in the mouth or with our legs. If his impulsion drops, we ask him one more time with our legs and, if that is not sufficient, we apply the schooling whip with increasing intensity until it makes him move forwards. After which, we make a big fuss of him, bringing him back to walk, and then start all over again. If the horse does not want to go into trot, we ask again with a light pressure of our legs. If this is not sufficient, we proceed with the schooling whip as described above. Once it has been established that the horse goes ahead willingly and maintains the gait, we can start to analyse the situation.

Leaving him to his own natural balance, with long reins and without contact (or just enough to be able to control direction), we look at his position.

In youngsters, we will normally be faced with a half-extended neck-line with the poll tending to open above the vertical. This is how the horse reacts to the weight and the imbalance brought about by the rider, with lines that tend to be concave instead of convex. Such an attitude, incapable of supporting the weight of the rider without creating repercussions to the bone structure of the vertebral column, should be corrected as soon as possible and now we know how.

We should expect a neck-line that is isn't perfectly straight, but which always tends to flex to one side. Even the horse's gaits will not be straight, with the shoulders always tending to fall in or go out, according to which rein he is on. In circles he will tend to go out or fall in always according to which rein he is on and as a consequence of his natural flexion. We shouldn't think for one moment about the haunches and should not try to make him straight; we can make little corrections of direction and nothing else as it is still too soon. We leave him to get

Julie de Joncaire Narten, our translator, on Ulisse di Reschio.

used to carrying our weight first and then start by taking up contact with the headcollar and then gently with the bit. Attention: contact and nothing else.

We have previously taught our horse lateral and vertical flexions on the headcollar in a static manner (still), now our objective is to have a horse who is relaxed and available to our requests of the hand on the headcollar on its own, without the associations of de-contraction of the bit on his jaw; he won't be up to it.

We should start to ask for vertical flexions on the headcollar, trying to maintain a light contact on the bit. Slowly, the bit will have a more active role than the headcollar. I repeat, the advantage will be noticeable both during the gradual passing from the bit to the headcollar and vice versa. In the meantime we should ask him every so often to make some large circles and change of rein. If, when we change rein, we get the impression that we are riding a horse with different characteristics, we shouldn't worry too much, it is a normal symptom of his asymmetry.

As we did from standstill, once we have established the contact, we should apply a light increasing pressure on the headcollar, and if his reply is the one we hoped for (yielding to the request), we can proceed as we know how. If it is not, we absolutely should not let it be a problem, or think that we haven't done our groundwork properly. Let's remember that things change under movement, and carry on maintaining pressure. But pressure on the headcollar can't be intensified or maintained for very long, it's not our aim to make the horse heavy. Therefore, maintaining pressure on the headcollar, we also augment it with that of the bit, increasing the stimuli to search for the reactive signals of the horse. Now we will 'only' need sensitivity to identify the correct reaction, after which we proceed with the simultaneous de-contraction, reverting to contact with the headcollar, taking our hands forward, inducing the horse to follow them. If this were not to happen, then we should immediately re-start – from the beginning. If we grasp the horse's intention to do and we work on that, it will be a fantastic experience. It depends on us.

Should the horse give opposition to the bit, we remember not to work too much on the bars of the mouth but on the corner, maintaining the pressure but changing the point of request.

Our objective will be that of inducing the horse to seek contact with our hands through de-contractive associations.

Never accept heaviness or non-reaction as the norm, because it isn't. If stimuli of the bit are required, they should be made without delay. If reactive stimuli are required the correct actions should be carried out. Be careful what, when and how you ask it, just as you should pay the greatest attention to every variation of the horse's state, always encouraging the correct associations.

The horse's mind will always be ready to find solutions of stability, but never concede passive reaction. If the headcollar is used badly, it can encourage the horse into a comfort zone based on non-reaction. Lightness should always be a choice on the part of the horse, but we must supply him with the correct elements to be able to make such choices.

We must never permit the horse to give too strong a reply on the headcollar. Releasing a pressure (yielding) that makes the horse heavy on the headcollar and then de-contracting him on the bit (in a following moment, disconnected from the action), is a mistake at the grammatical level. (It is equally wrong to do the same thing with only the bit.) Once the pressure is given (the request is made), it should not be interrupted or lightened unless there is a positive response. If the horse tends not to respond quickly, or to stiffen, we should de-contract him on the bit but without first releasing the pressure on the headcollar. We should do both things together and then effect the yielding with both together. An error in grammatical form will not bear fruit.

The correct use of the language will be fundamental. Always.

If the horse tends to force our hands too far forwards or low, regardless of the correctness of our actions, it will be important to request a de-contraction or, if necessary, use the half-halt with a lively vibration on the bit high and not on the bars of the mouth and without using our legs ('hands without legs and legs without hands') and then lengthen the reins immediately the action is finished (descente de main).

The same response should be used for attempts at going beyond the vertical.

These defences by the horse can occur and should not be tolerated. Investigate their causes! If they are caused by bad communication, we must concentrate on finding a remedy as quickly as possible. Correction is often required as perfection does not reside in either us or them. Let's just try to remain vigilant to the defences induced by us.

Educational short-cuts do not exist; there are no facilities to help with an almost correct language. We must express our intentions clearly and equally clearly reward correct answers. Either we express ourselves really well or we must resort to constraint. Changing the procedure changes the results.

If our communication is correct, it will also be very, very efficient. No instrument exists that can equal the willingness of the horse to 'do'. His reactivity will grow in an exponential manner through the stimuli of an efficient communication. The question is: will we be capable to keep up with his progress?

Mental and physical dynamism will inevitably become our strength. We shouldn't always expect the same response; shouldn't fossilize our mind in mechanical repetitiveness. If we carry out a series of well-executed requests, we should expect a series of replies in a crescendo of reactions. If we are not ready to ask for de-contraction in time, or we are not ready to reduce our pressures suddenly on the basis of a more immediate response, it will be a problem.

The horse learns and we must do likewise.

To give an example, let's use our request to bring the horse's head on to the vertical. Applying a pressure we have a response. If the response were initially to come to five hundred grams of pressure in three seconds, a repeat of the same would quickly bring the horse to create associations which will shorten the time of reaction in his attempt to find a comfort zone as soon as possible. Therefore, after a while, for the same request, we will have a reduction both in the pressure 'two hundred grams' as well as in the reaction time 'two seconds'.

Our ability to grasp such intention on the part of the horse will be our gratification: the prize for us and for him. All these techniques are required in that we must manage to base our timing on the horse's intention to do. This is the road to lightness.

The more that our requests to follow our hands are further from the natural position of the horse, the more time he requires to create mental associations and appropriate physical reactions. If the horse has a reversed neck-line, he will need more time before he rounds and maintains such a shape in a stable manner (muscle memory). Even his attempts to lean on our requests will be stronger, as will be his attempts to return to a position that is more natural to him, but not correct.

Corrective gymnastics can, at times, become complicated both for the horse and the rider; this is normal. Patience is required; the muscular apparatus of the horse will adapt as much as possible to the changes and will find stability in time. Let's remember that a de-contraction will only be efficient if the hand is ready to go towards the horse's mouth at the very moment of the de-contraction, even just a little, but it must yield. Without this it will all be useless.

Of course, all of this refers in particular to the initial stages of de-contraction. Subsequently we will apply an ever-greater number of variables, like for example, gently closing our fingers

Maria Francesca Patrizi on Punto di Reschio: Spanish walk, a useful exercise.

asking the jaw to de-contract, making the poll turn, following our movements and ready to receive further instructions. In practice the horse's jaw should follow our hand either when open or closed (not contracted, not over-flexed) whether that is in the act of going away, following or coming towards the hand, always maintaining contact and lightness. The *mise en main* is the action of the horse seeking contact with an educated hand that tends to educate.

When we ask our horse to round his neck-line and to bring his head close to the vertical, we should not expect immediate stability, but a position that will tend to be stable in time (more or less short, according to the muscular difficulty he has in holding such a position).

Therefore, we proceed to ask, yield, ask, yield, ask, yield … trying to shorten the times of the requests, adapting ourselves to the reactivity of the response and, as a consequence, increasing the time of stability in the comfort zone (the one which we requested) and effecting immediate pressure every time that the horse tends to go out of position (uncomfortable zone). The more we anticipate the horse's attempt to change by means of a pressure, the sooner we will have stability. The correct timing for a request (for a horse who tends to go out of position) and the yielding (when the horse returns to de-contraction) should always have our maximum attention.

Your hand should be your horse's best friend and your greatest ally. Work carried out well will bring your horse to follow your hand and search out your contact, associating this with a comfort zone; a place where he likes to be. Consistency and understanding: consistency and understanding.

Let's remember that all horses will tend towards stability. If this doesn't happen quickly, even if it were to be an inconsistent stability, then it means that there is something wrong.

LATERAL FLEXION

One hears many theories on lateral flexions of the neck, some of which are truly absurd. One of these, probably the most common, insists on affirming that a lateral flexion of the neck should never exceed that of the dorso-lumbosacral tract (that is, the arc of curvature that

Carlotta De Biagi on Eva (student instructor FEEL course).

the horse is able to achieve with his back, from the withers to the haunches). Such a theory is known as 'curvature of the whole'. The absurdity of such a theory, which unfortunately many practise, is that of limiting the flexion of such a mobile part as the horse's neck to a much less mobile part; the vertebral column. If it is a contracted horse that we want, then surely this is the correct route. Thinking of this reminds me of my first toy robot when I was a child, which tried to imitate humanoid movements with poor success.

Personally, I try to refer back to what is anatomically compatible with the natural mobility of the horse. The neck is equipped with enormous mobility; it can bend itself 180° – the vertebral column (dorso-lumbosacral tract) absolutely cannot. There is only one part of the latter he can extend, which is equipped with limited lateral mobility.

Many confuse the horse's ability to achieve lateral engagement of the hind legs with the flexibility of the lumbosacral tract, associating to one the merits of the other to sustain their own theory. The leg cannot flex the back – if anything it can create more engagement. Anatomy is a much more exact science than the rules to which many would like to adapt the mechanics of the horse. If a rule goes against such scientifically proven anatomical principles, then intellect would require that it be changed. But that will never happen. The obtuseness of rules is stronger than reason. Always.

The mobility of the neck, when used well, brings such enormous benefits that to limit its use is simply stupid. Without entering too much into specifics, it is right to learn that lateral flexions of the neck do not bring benefits just to the neck. All parts of the horse, and in particular the dorso-lumbosacral tract, lengthen or de-contract, acquiring harmonic dynamism. Thanks to flexions in fact, a lengthening of the external muscular fascia occurs (convex side), including the part of the ileo-spinal (dorso-lumbosacral), whilst it de-contracts the concave part. To be correct we should say that it's thanks to the de-contraction of the concave part that there is a lengthening of the convex part and not vice versa, which all stems from the de-contrac-

Flexion and counter-flexion.

tion. Also, the flexion mechanically contains the inside shoulder, favouring a broader action than that of the outside, the hind leg on the convex side will tend to thrust more than it engages whilst that of the concave side will engage more than it thrusts. This is really useful for re-establishing balance or to start to make the horse straight, and we are not talking about work on two tracks, but of flexion of the neck made with a minimum of awareness.

But what is the basis of pronounced lateral flexion of the neck?

It is simply that kind of gymnastics practised by all athletes regardless of their type of sport: 'stretching'.

There does not exist in the world an athlete who does not practise this with assiduous regularity and, since I see my horse as an athlete, as a good trainer, I consider stretching an active part of my programme.

For the purpose of carrying out gymnastics in order to arrive at an efficient flexion, we need to start to understand the control of the horse's shoulders .

Up until now, we have linked direction to the horse's poll: that is, changing its position and directing it on the path we want, taking it for granted that the whole horse will follow. In achieving this, the inside rein will have played the main role.

But now that our athlete has started to take our weight with more ease, with a stable extension of the neck, keeping his head close to the vertical, the moment has arrived to disassociate the direction of the horse's head from his directional movement. In fact we should start to see and direct the shoulders independently of the change of position of the head or the bending of the neck. This is not easy and hardly instinctive for us, but it is indispensable for the athletic horse.

Another tricky thing will be that of starting to guide the horse using only the outside rein. By outside rein we always mean the one that is opposite to the flexion of the neck, independently of which rein we are on, or motional direction of the horse.

As the inside rein has the task of flexing or directing the head, the outside rein should do all the rest. It will be its job to direct the shoulders and to receive the channelled energy of the horse.

One could say that if movement is the essence of equitation, the outside rein is what controls it.

The inside rein could help the outside rein, but never the contrary. The horse is guided with the outside rein and the sooner we start to fix this concept in our brain, the better. Work on two tracks will make all this more visible, but it is necessary for the proper execution of stretching.

Starting from the principle of the horse being correctly on the bit, we must imagine the outside rein as a joystick capable of directing the shoulders.

Before starting flexions we need a few more details.

- Every time we speak of de-contraction we must understand that this must start in the first place from the jaw and then spread to all of the horse. So, until the horse associates such de-contraction with the request on the headcollar, the bit must play its part.
- Make sure that the headcollar is never too tight, that it always allows the jaw the movement of de-contraction.

The horse who is naturally flexed right will, in a straight line, have the following more or less accentuated characteristics. On the right rein, he will tend to maintain the track, bringing his shoulder towards the manège wall (escaping towards the outside), with his head and haunches turned towards the inside. Remedy this with a light flexion towards the outside

Casanova di Reschio: passage.

tends to bring the shoulders towards the inside realigning them with the haunches. We do not yet have the means to work on the haunches, so we have to align the shoulders.

On the left rein, he will try to abandon the track, coming to the inside, and will have the tendency to carry his head and haunches towards the outside. Remedy this with a pronounced left flexion; the base of the neck pushes the shoulders towards the right, realigning them with the haunches.

On a circle on the left rein, the horse will turn through 'loss of balance' turning his head towards the outside and falling on the inside shoulder, tending to make the circle smaller. Remedy this with pronounced left flexion and a circle that tends to get bigger.

On a circle on the right rein, natural flexion pushes the shoulder towards the outside, enlarging the circle. The right foreleg will step a shorter distance than normal, hampered also by the way he has turned his head. The left foreleg will tend to open up in support of the excursion of the shoulders. To remedy this, we must limit the excursion of the shoulders towards the outside with a left counter-flexion.

Besides this we must add a principle to be followed for the different types of neck-line conformations.

- **Attached low, short and thick:** The most complex to deal with. Horses with this conformation tend to contract, seeking a strong downward leaning on the hand; they don't like to carry themselves. Half-halts carried out well, followed by or anticipated by a sudden de-contraction of the jaw will be the rule. We would rarely ask for a complete extension of the neck, rather it would be desirable if it shortened. Be careful to always maintain lightness after every request, gradually increasing the time in which the horse tends to carry himself in a correct manner. This requires an expert hand that does not delay too much when the horse tries to lean strongly. Lateral flexions are great for this type, or to bring the poll forwards, but be careful that downward extensions are not too pronounced.

- **Reversed neck-line:** This type of neck-line, usually slender and long and softly attached, often has a notable level of mobility of the poll. The sensation will be that the horse's mouth tends to escape from the hand, carrying itself upwards in an unstable manner. The de-contraction of the jaw at the appropriate angle with the head tending towards the vertical, will bring the neck-line to round itself, re-establishing balance. We must often ensure that the horse seeks our hand; the stable contact must be our prerogative, in that the notable mobility of the poll will put our reaction to follow the mouth to the test. Such a horse will willingly carry out even pronounced flexions, but we must be careful that he only does this with his head on the vertical and that he seeks the contact with our hand. He must seek our hand.

- **Hyperflexed:** This is an attitude induced by countless mishaps. In nature, such characteristics only exist for short moments. It is not an intrinsic characteristic of the horse, but one of his ways of defence. A hyperflexed horse is a horse who has suffered much, who has endured human ambitions in the worst way. He has not been understood, respected or loved. He has given up his own dignity. If you think that I am exaggerating, it is may be because you don't know the methods used so that a horse is constrained to assume such a position. We must wake up his natural attitudes by taking some steps backward. Light contact, half-halts and sudden opening of the reins, trying to stimulate the horse to trust our hands again and seek contact with them. Work with him open and never closed, suddenly vibrating the hand every time that he tries to avoid it, and yielding generously when he tries to seek a forward contact. Once we have re-established a true and stable contact, we should proceed according to his anatomical type. A hyperflexed horse is also a horse with a limited field of vision caused by this position, which is another irrefutable reason contrasting the theory of those who would bestow naturalness to this barbaric condition. To be vigilant is one of the prime necessities of herds animals: the auto-privation of this condition would not be amongst the horse's intentions.

Irrecoverable horses do not exist, only those that are not understood. Let's remember always that a horse is capable of changing his attitudes in response to his change of conditions.

A shoulder in with Matilde Radicchi on Il Magnifico di Reschio.

We should ask horses to do what we want through explaining and speaking in the correct manner.

All this work should be carried out a stage at a time, preparing the musculature of the horse to get used to positions which are different from those which he has a propensity to assume naturally. Assuming that it is clear what we have to do, as always we will have to deal with how to do it.

For lateral flexions, the same rules always apply. Requests are made in the same way. The only changes are in the differences of the positions, but the method of request is always the same. The basis is always the need to grasp the horse's intention of 'doing'.

Let's use an example of a circle on the left rein with a horse who is naturally flexed right. We must seek a pronounced left flexion. In doing so, we will encounter the natural resistance of the horse, where he will react to our request for flexion by falling even more into the circle, or trying to implement vertical yielding. In these circumstances, the outside rein should be activated, opening and opposing this tendency, seeking to enlarge the circle whilst maintaining flexion.

Now, if we try to make a complete circle with a pronounced flexion or even simply with a balanced flexion when dealing with a young horse, it means that what we have done up until now has served no purpose.

Remember, '1+1+1+1+1 ….' is always our way of proceeding, especially when we confront new exercises. In the case of the above-mentioned exercise, we should yield, with a light flexion (inside rein), through the request on the outside rein, if the horse doesn't increase the size of the circle, but stops for a second to fall into it. Repeating this will indicate to the horse the road we wish him to follow and he will be quite happy to establish a different balance. We must make him do what we want through explaining and speaking in the correct language. For youngsters or horses unaccustomed to this type of exercise, we should be patient with them in order to arrive at stable continuity, but not if they don't have the intention to do it. The horse will immediately understand if we initially make our yielding the moment he does it; keep the exercise going for longer, always ready to reward him for his attempts even when he is rather unclear what we are asking.

Strengthen the 'desire to do with' with 'doing' itself.

Contact, requests on the headcollar or the bit, de-contraction, timing, knowledge and consistency are and must always be our tools. We don't need anything else and, above all, the horses don't need anything else and, moreover they don't deserve anything else.

They just need our understanding and our proficiency.

Appendix: FEEL

THE STRUCTURE OF FEEL

The idea of FEEL has been around for more than twenty years, but it only became a reality in 2014. Having said that, we would like to point out that FEEL is the only private Italian school to be recognized by a national riding federation (FITETREC) and FEEL instructors are equated with first level federal instructors. Not only this, but the FEEL method has been integrated and will be an important part of the training of federal instructors.

Why FITETREC? Because, as I wrote in the book, life is made up of encounters. I met the President of the Federation, Avv. Alessandro Silvestri, and whilst not being a horseman in the strict sense of the word, he proved to be a very sensitive person and intellectually prepared, in understanding what FEEL was trying to achieve. He was, amongst other things, a very 'practical' man.' I still remember his words, which were: 'If indeed you are able to do what you claim, we would be happy to welcome you into the Federation'. I only now realize, knowing him a little better, that this was not skepticism, but rather wanting to see something concrete.

This is just to reiterate the validity of what we do. FEEL qualifications are divided into:

- Student instructors
- First level instructors
- Second level instructors
- Third level instructors
- Trainers
- Integration of pony activities

The training of a student instructor lasts at least ten months, which is the time required to get to the right level to pass the exams of a first level instructor. Before the theoretical/practical exam, the student has to have participated with his own horse(s) for a minimum of four courses, each four days long in which the following subjects are dealt with:

- Communication between man and horse
- Work in liberty
- Work on the lunge
- On the bit (contact)
- Study of the positions (extension)
- Basic gymnastics (extensions, flexions, counter-flexions in all three gaits).
- Teaching skills
- Studies of the classics
- Veterinary knowledge (anatomy)
- Functional anatomy

At the exam the student must present a thesis on the subjects dealt with during the course, and will be evaluated, not only on his ability to interact with his horse by achieving fixed goals, but also his ability to know how to pass on to others what he has learned, the level of culture in the various subjects and the indispensable commitment to apply the behavioural ethics of FEEL. Failure to comply with the ethics of FEEL or the use of coercive instruments such as unsuitable bits, martingales, return reins etc. leads to immediate suspension or revocation of the qualification, regardless of the reasons. The student instructor cannot give lessons to others without the physical presence of a first level instructor. The FEEL instructors, from the first level and up, must demonstrate their ability to communicate appropriately with the aid of just the head collar, just the bit and with both, the correct associations for de-contracting the horse.

There is no maximum time limit to take the exams. Once the mandatory course has been attended it is possible to request private lessons from other FEEL instructors or trainers and to take the necessary time for an adequate preparation. It is possible to repeat the whole course for that level the following year (as audience), and without further cost.

At the second level, as well as studying the topics covered in more depth, work on two tracks will be introduced in both extended and raised positions, flying canter changes and the principles of collection.

At the third level, students will face collected work; piaffe, passage, pirouettes, and the introduction to jumping.

After having completed the third level, students can enter the course for trainers. Trainers can organize courses for students and can issue FEEL diplomas for first, second and third levels even in countries other than Italy, operating within the current rules for that country.

The integration of pony activities is a course that will help instructors in training young or very young riders with specific technical teaching. The course can only be entered after the completion of the first level.

Two words on FITETREC

The Italian Federation of Equestrian Tourism Trec Ante, founded in Rome in 1968, recognized by and associated with CONI (Italian National Olympic Committee), is today a point of reference for national and international equitation. It is made up of regional committees, has 700 affiliated and integrated centres and has to date issued more than 25,000 licences.

The objectives of the Federation, currently guided by its President Alessandro Silvestri, are divided on two fronts: that of the expansion, evaluation and promotion of equestrian tourism, recognized as an extraordinary means of exploring the territories, art and culture of our country, and that of organizing and developing equestrian disciplines with relative competitions and national and international championships tied to the countryside and work with the horse.

FORMATION OF ETHOLOGY AND EQUITATION IN LIGHTNESS

The idea was born a long time ago, during the time when we were experimenting with the techniques of the headcollar and the bit. It was just an uncertain and confused idea, but little by little it took form and substance. Now, thanks to the will of a lot of people, it is a concrete and tangible reality. To say that it wasn't easy is a banality, just as I always risk being banal every time I speak of FEEL. perhaps because of the people who form the structure, perhaps

FEEL instructors.

for their ideas, the principles, I don't know. What I do know is that it is part of my life that has brought me to know fantastic realities and people whom I could not do without. You can like it or not but one thing certain is that FEEL is made from the heart and with the best sentiments of many people; it has no commercial structure, just a philosophical one, which aims to enrich the culture of many and not the finances of the few.

FEEL has always worked, seeking to develop techniques aimed at enhancing the methods of communication between human and horse, studying the language and trying to translate it into a grammatical form with set rules – that is, rules that can be explained and understood in the same methodology used for the study of foreign languages. All this has led, over the years, to the confirmation of results through the use of non-coercive instruments in our approach with the horse. The transparency of execution must never be illusionary, and the simplicity of the use of the headcollar must never create excuses for non-execution. Achieving efficacy in complex exercises, through the use of simple instruments, bringing communicative capacity to the maximum, keeping coercion to a minimum. That is what we do.

The attainment of such results, which are clearly not simple would, however, not be possible if, in addition to the study of the language, we did not include the understanding of the dynamics of movement in the variables of the biodiversity of the species.

The language, even if fundamental, would be useless without the help of many more elements that go to complete the entirety of what a horse is, always considering these elements in relation to what the horse does and in relation to preparing him for what he has to do.

Irene Boriosi with Maestoso (student instructor FEEL).

Silvia Montanucci on Hebreo (student instructor FEEL).

Approximation and simplification have always been enemies against which we need to be on our guard. Efficient and sincere results are our best allies.

We do not offer short-cuts, but something precious that can help mankind in an evolutionary journey towards interaction with the horse. We seek to give everyone the necessary instruments in order that they may communicate with efficiency, raising their own potential to reach a collaboration between rider and horse based on reciprocal respect, and on the fundamental assumption that one respects what one is.

Seeking to change a human, transforming them into a horse in order can become a part of the herd, is not our aim. Neither is seeking to make horses take on human expression – that is, those more understandable to us.

We belong to a historic period in which the sudden arrival of ethology has brought many good changes. But the belief that a horse is not perfectly capable of recognizing an omnivore biped who is seeking to impersonate them, risks distorting all that a good ethological approach could bring. We cannot be part of their herd, but we can, of course, seek to understand their way of expressing themselves, in an attempt to establish a communication that puts us in the condition of being understood. Respect what one is, whether human or horse, without upsetting nature; theirs or ours.

Training

Divided into various parts, its objective is the study of the grammatical structure of the language of horses. From this springs the learning of body language and of its expressive potential in the initial stages of work from the ground.

Another phase of training is the transposition of body language to the mounted horse. This is one of the cardinal points of this education; to preserve the efficiency of 'imprinting' even when we are in the saddle. This is that delicate moment when our language, our use of grammar in instructions, must change without upsetting its structure.

The training will include an analysis of the functional anatomy of the horse and of the biodiversity of the species. This will involve general notions of how a horse works and an analysis of horses' prevalent types of structural and functional construction.

Hence will follow the study of gymnastics based on the type of horse, and its direct appli-

Julie de Joncaire Narten (student instructor, FEEL).

cation through the language of execution. Gymnastics has as its indispensable objective the well-being of the horse and his preservation over time. These exercises aim to develop the appropriate musculature and balance to enable the horse to carry the rider and the rider to lead the horse. Language will serve as the basis of all this. We are not tied to any particular discipline. We do not wish to form part of any particular category other than to the one to which all people who love horses more than their ego belong.

The word 'FEEL' itself means to amplify our knowledge and understanding of the horse, feeling and perceiving that all this will bring about an improvement simply by being together.

This is what we want, what we need: 'FEEL', the well-being of our horse every time we enter into contact with him.

Ethology

Irrespective of the school of thought from which it derives, it is impossible to be unaware to what extent the efficiency of work from the ground (imprinting), sees a sharp decline in its expressive power when the horse is mounted.

The reason for this is not to be found in its basic grammatical structure (which is always identical) but in the actual grammar available to the rider once in the saddle, which lacks the means of expression that are available during work on the ground.

Clearly, working from the ground or mounting imply different actions and involvement for the rider. Obvious? Perhaps, but we believe that, in order to maintain an ethological linguistic root, the direct emotional involvement entered into when mounting a horse requires a philosophy, an approach, which originates from the assumption that for us, for our physique, for our mind, mounting a horse is not natural, just as it is not natural for the horse to be mounted.

Neither of us has been created for that purpose.

Having ascertained and accepted all this, we can search for a valid compromise based on both the horses' and our adaptability, which has developed during evolution.

We must slightly change the key to understanding, see things in a transparent manner and not let them be clouded by the mist of emotion that often leads us to fail to see reality simply because the observation point is different. When we are in the saddle our movements are tied to those of the horse, our certainty depends on the ability to communicate. If we lose our lucidity, if we lose the awareness of what we are doing, both our safety and that of the horse is at risk.

The visual information that our brain receives no longer only involves the images of the horse moving at ease at liberty with us easily moving about on the ground. Things change radically in the saddle and, in order to recognize the attitudes and relate them to what we are feeling without centre of balance becomes fundamental. In the saddle everything changes; the way movement is perceived, our balance and the horse's balance, the manner in which we perceive the horse …. The communicative root should not, however, change.

We must develop an ethological grammar in execution which allows us to disassociate our physical being from intentionality and then re-associate these aspects again.

We must communicate efficiently in movement; succeed in expressing ourselves in the saddle as efficiently as on the ground.

To achieve all this both we and the horse need to feel understood and at ease.

We seek out harmony in unnatural movements, mastering them through cohesion, both physical and in terms of expressive syntax; never damaging reciprocal respect.

Equitation

Art is an array of emotional shapes, whether physical (sculpture) or conceptual (poetry). Poetry, for example, has a form, a structure we are easily able to distinguish from an instruction manual. However, not all of us will be able to feel

*Naomi Statuti with Dorado
(student instructor FEEL).*

ts beauty. This will depend from the innumerable variables that have gone to form our char-acter: genetics, experience, and so on. We will nonetheless be able to recognize its form, whether it is able to move us or not.

Now, putting art aside for the moment, we have tried to develop an equitation based on recognizable geometrical shapes, which fit that particular type of horse, that moment and that exercise.

To be able to recognize the requirements of that horse, either to correct a fault or improve a strength in that exercise, is crucial. The more we are able to make the horse assume shapes or positions which are correct for that type, that moment and that exercise … the more we will notice its efficiency.

An extended horse has a different shape from a collected one. It may seem the usual plati-tude but, if seen in the complexity of the variables in the structure, in the attitudes, of the type of horse, it becomes difficult to execute. The ability to understand the need, and consequently make that particular horse adopt the correct shape at the right moment in the right exercise, is the difference between assisting and hindering the horse in his execution.

Hence the correctness in 'making the horse execute', carried out through the correct language, is nothing other than making the horse assume the correct position appropriate to preparing him to execute our requests by progressive gymnastics. To mould the horse's shape in a constructive manner allows us to develop balance, musculature and willingness to execute.

A long, thin neck (to make a simple example) will require a certain type of gymnastics and the horse will need to assume positions (shapes) that are completely different from the ones required for a horse with a short, thick neck. Applying all this to different morphological structures, the complexity of the variables will become evident. To have the power to make the horse assume positions different from the appropriate ones does not, therefore, mean helping him.

To understand the need for the anatomical study of the dynamics of equine movement, and only thereafter adapt the positions to the morphological type by using an ethological language will help the horse. We will not achieve this by forcing him to adopt positions by coercive instruments (our hands can be such instruments), but only by seeking the collabora-tion of the horse in every phase of work through understanding and communication.

Obviously, not all of us will become poets, but with the right know-how we will nonetheless have the chance to become good technicians.

This is our vision of equitation, irrespective of the discipline which is practised. [This is fine as a principle, and the author and his followers are clearly more concerned with how they ride than with adherence to any discipline – which also fine – but perhaps it would be fair to mention to readers that the headcollar/bit arrangement promoted in these pages would not be permitted currently in official dressage competitions (certainly in UK), and it may be that it wouldn't be permitted in other competitive disciplines.]

Lightness

Wide use is being made of this word, which was reintroduced by maestro Philippe Karl [he was certainly a leading figure in popularizing the concept, but not the only one] in our present time (and there was indeed a great need for this), but this use is often distorted by misunder-standing and does little for equitation.

This is not an objective to be reached in an advanced stage of work. The concept that the horse is not yet ready for it is false. To believe that lightness is only achievable after long preparatory sessions of work is absurd.

It is equally absurd to have the horse do very little, leaving him in his natural equilibrium and waiting for him to be ready.... That horse will never be ready and his lightness will be inversely proportionate to our requests in the sense that 'the less he does the better off he is'. We could easily just put him out to pasture and, provided there aren't too many insects he would certainly be serene, light and in harmony with the world. But, not with us, in work.

Lightness resides in the clarity of the language and in the understanding of the needs of the horse in the specific phases of work.

Lightness is an attitude, a way of asking, of acting and of 'making him execute'. The root of lightness resides in the language we adopt and in the exercises of progressive gymnastics so as to prepare the horse for a continuous and harmonious evolution. It is not an objective to be achieved; it is a technique that should always be applied whenever we relate with horses. It is forever from the very first steps. Lightness resides in the very nature of horses, in their attitudes and in their communication; it is their communicative and evolutionary basis.

We don't need to look for it, it is already there. To understand it, learn to practise and live it in our daily dealings with them, this is indeed useful.

Lightness in equitation is the only instrument that the rider has to possess to make it beautiful, harmonious, pleasing to the eye and above all, pleasant to practise so as to render it as close as possible to an artistic expression. It may seem something delicate, a tender bud to be cultivated with care, but it is stronger than it appears and its solid roots dig deep into the very essence of horses.

They will always be ready for lightness in its every form. Will we?

Behavioural Ethics

The principal aim of the association and of the courses is the propagation and development of all those parameters that increase the psychological and physical well-being of the horse.

The purchase of a horse or the decision to interact with one is a choice. Taking care of him and behaving appropriately through the understanding of his needs is a duty towards the horse.

All those who intend to interact with a horse have the moral duty to learn the techniques that enable them to develop a relationship based on correct and coherent ethological communication.

Recently, the parameters of equitation have changed drastically. These changes have not occurred out of concern for the well-being of the horse, but from exploitation and coercion aimed at achieving sporting results without the slightest concern for the horse's needs, reducing him to a simple 'means' to an end. Too many horses have and continue to pay the price. Insane competition based on ethologically unacceptable concepts has resulted in horrors such as 'hyperflexion', tight nosebands and so on which, instead of being eradicated, have been rewarded in international competitions, thereby offering the public a questionable result achieved through debatable means. Coercion has been established as an acceptable method to the detriment of understanding and respect. Clearly, words such as 'lightness' and 'harmony' are used with complete disregard to their meaning in their practical application.

Hence FEEL's choice to propagate methods based on the understanding between human and horse.

The Horse's Rights:
The horse is entitled to have a person caring for him or interacting with him with the following characteristics:

- Understanding of the basic physiological needs (size of paddock, size of box, nutrition, socialization and so on.
- Understanding of the musculoskeletal system so as to avoid making absurd requests and putting the horse in impossible situations.
- Understanding of the most frequent ailments to which horses are subject.
- Understanding of how the horse expresses himself and learning of the appropriate language.
- Understanding of non-coercive techniques in daily work able to develop collaboration in learning free from constraints based on a human's behavioural ignorance.
- Understanding of the use of tack according to one's horse.
- Understanding ....

The horse asks to be understood before being 'used'. A horse is a social animal and needs to relate with humans. Humans have the duty to establish a relationship based on reciprocal respect.

All members of FEEL and, in particular, instructors or student instructors have a duty to: practise and propagate a correct ethical behaviour principally based on the needs of the horse and aimed at establishing with him a relationship based on reciprocal understanding.

www.doyouspeakequis.com

Index

Pages numbers in italic indicate illustrations covered by the text.